Essential Succulents

essential
succulents
THE BEGINNER'S GUIDE

Ken Shelf

PHOTOGRAPHY BY RACHEL WEILL

callisto
publishing
an imprint of Sourcebooks

Published by Callisto Publishing LLC C/O Sourcebooks LLC
P.O. Box 4410, Naperville, Illinois 60567-4410
(630) 961-3900
callistopublishing.com

Printed and bound in China
OGP 2

To my Mom and Dad.
Thanks for nurturing me with water and sun, and then letting me grow wild, with minimal manicuring and regular maintenance.

CONTENTS

INTRODUCTION

What is a succulent? It's not a scientific term, but rather a description of plants that store water in their leaves, stems, or roots. Most have evolved in challenging landscapes where they must rely on themselves to survive. I first witnessed their incredible fortitude during the 1994 holiday season, when a friend gifted me a *Haworthia fasciata*. I still have it today! Beyond its resilience, I marveled at its gorgeous stripes that looked like frosting, and the delicate flower that opened at the end of its long stem. Soon after, my wife Amy, and I began collecting cacti, aloes, and aeoniums in planters on our rooftop deck in San Francisco. We were awed by the saturated blacks, greens, and yellows of the Aeonium 'Sunburst' and *Aeonium arboreum* 'Zwartkop,' and wowed by the tubular, red-orange flowers that sprouted from our Fan Aloe. We loved to sit on our rooftop in the afternoon sun and simply enjoy the company of these plants.

When we opened our succulent shop, we decided to call it Succulence to evoke the richness of life embodied in these hardy plants. I was fascinated with Opalina, whose flesh nearly defies description, with swirling pigments of blue, green, purple, and pink dancing like watercolors beneath a frosty surface, and whose star-shaped yellow blooms have the most improbable red triangles on their tips. As I began to make **vertical garden** (see Glossary) art with succulents, I became enthralled with their willingness to live in all sorts of environments. I crafted succulent terrariums and small container gardens that entranced me with their miniature beauty. When I was asked if I could replicate them on a large scale, I obtained a California state contractor's license and began landscaping outdoor succulent gardens for many of my clients. Over the years, I have planted sedums and senecios to fill planting beds, and cactus and Red Yucca as stand-alone focal points. I saw *Agave attenuata* withstand direct sun, and gasterias and haworthias thrive in partial shade. I became passionate about these "will-to-live" plants and their architectural forms, admirable strength for survival, and natural ability to defy drought and neglect.

Since we opened the shop in 2009, Succulence has become an established destination for San Francisco plant lovers. My staff and I have taught hundreds of workshops, created countless centerpieces for weddings and fund-raising events, and brought succulents into our clients' homes and offices through custom plantings and landscaping services.

I am thrilled to be able to share my succulent knowledge with you in this book. We begin with information about 50 easy-to-grow succulents, then move on to a basic understanding of these plants, how to care for them indoors and outside, and how to propagate them and design with them. I also provide you with eight easy DIY projects to help cultivate your skills, confidence, and creativity. My aim is to empower you on your succulent-growing journey. After reading this book, you will have all the know-how you need to keep these plants alive and healthy. Then the real fun begins!

Chapter One

THE 50 BEST SUCCULENT VARIETIES FOR BEGINNERS

One of the greatest things about succulents is that you can grow and enjoy them no matter where you live. Many can thrive outdoors in extreme weather conditions, and some can live happily indoors as houseplants. Some will grow very large; agaves can send out a flower that might reach 25 feet tall. Others, like the Gasteria Dwarf Tongue, may never exceed

5 inches. As landscape greenery, succulents use less water than other plant varieties and provide bold, artistic imagery for you and your neighbors. They are also excellent housemates, not needing much more than a passing hello every week or two, and providing you with steady companionship and occasionally pretty flowers. Succulents are great plants to grow and admire, but their value doesn't end there. Some are used as medicines or for fire safety; some are made into beverages or even eaten as food.

In this chapter, you'll find a collection of 50 easy-to-grow, easy-to-find hardy succulents that can thrive in a variety of regions. I want your confidence and skill level to grow along with them, so I've provided 11 categories of information for each plant, including a care guide and even arrangement tips. Paired with knowledge of your indoor and outdoor environment, this guide will provide all you need to choose the proper plants for any growing situation. Scan the guide to determine what's appropriate based on your hardiness zone, where you will be planting, and how much sun and water the plants will need. I've also provided facts about each plant's geographic origins, tips for cultivation, and what kind of flowers each one will produce and when. My goal is to get you as excited about succulents as I am. Follow my instructions, and don't be afraid to experiment. Sometimes we learn from things that don't work out. The important thing is to enjoy the process. Your succulent lifestyle awaits.

SUCCULENT BASICS

Succulents don't require a whole lot of care. Though it may seem counterintuitive, they are actually stronger when neglected. It is easy to "over care" for them by providing too much water or fertilizer. There are some variations in the care required for these plants, but many general rules apply. Familiarize yourself with the basic guidelines below and you'll soon become a confident succulent cultivator. We will go into greater details on care in chapter 2.

Watering can be kept to a minimum. Many succulent families emerged in areas of extreme drought and can exist for long periods in that state. In general, succulents would much rather be underwatered than overwatered. Container gardens, including any plants that are not planted directly in the ground, need to be watered by hand or through an irrigation system. Plants in the earth will start taking pretty good care of themselves by the time they fit in 6-inch pots. Smaller plants may need regular water until they are established.

Fertilization. A great attribute of succulents is their ability to withstand neglect. While other types of plants appreciate food and at times need it to continue to thrive, succulents evolved to take care of themselves. There is a term we use to describe the pretty colors that appear when succulents get extra sun, cold, or heat combined with a lack of water and fertilizer: stress. Fertilization can be required if your plant is in older or non-augmented soil, but it is not needed often. A rule of thumb is to feed succulents during the warm growth months that usually stretch from early spring through late fall, though some plants will grow in the colder months. An example of a winter-growing succulent is the aeonium, which is **dormant** (see Glossary) in summer.

Pruning and manicuring need only occur when you want to trim for appearance or propagation (see Glossary). In some cases, growth may be stunted when there are many branches on a plant, and that might be a time to prune. Manicuring is when you are pruning for shape. This cutting can be accomplished by pinching off bits with your fingers or a sharp pair of garden scissors below the rosette or set of leaves where the stem connects to a branch. An aeonium or aloe might require larger tools, such as shears or clippers. Euphorbias secrete a toxic sap, so wear gloves when pruning those plants.

Propagation is when you grow new plants from an existing one. This is part of the fun of succulents, which can often regrow themselves from just one leaf. Many of the plant families propagate differently, from leaves and cuttings to offsets and division. Try propagation when you want more plants for your home, gifts for friends, cuttings for plant art, or to clear the plant of excessive growth. You can also compost extra pieces that you don't use. See chapter 4 for more specific propagation instructions.

Acclimation. Succulents need to be slowly acclimated to bright light if they have spent months inside. So give them a little more light each day for a week or two before leaving them out in the heat completely. This will prevent sunburns on the leaves that won't heal.

ECHEVERIA 'BLUE ROSE'

Echeveria x imbricata

9–11; ideally 40°F–70°F;
however, they can survive
very brief cold spells
down to about 20°F.

IDEAL LIGHTING
Full sun, partial sun

GROWING LOCATION
Outside is best, though they
will grow inside in a bright
room with great sun.

SIZE
4-6" tall; 4-6"

Frequently grows hens and chicks–style **(see Glossary).**
Will fill up an area nicely; clumps in tight batches.
Mexican native, like all echeveria.

Special Features: Pretty light blue color with pinkish edges. Very dramatic when orange-red flowers bloom in sequence, yielding clumps of flowers for many weeks at a time.

Care Instructions: Outside: Very easy; needs little water and a soil that drains well. Indoors: water every two weeks; let dry between waterings.

Watch Out For: Without enough sun, most echeveria will grow tall and **leggy** (see Glossary) as they look for the light. If they get too much water, a rot could form under the soil that will kill the plant. Though they are pest-resistant, look out for mealybugs and aphids, especially if grown outside.

Arrangement Tips: Imbricata is fantastic in rock gardens and as a companion plant to trees and larger succulents like aloe and agave. These are good container garden plants, as they will fill up a space nicely with offsets over time. As they propagate, they will press up tightly against one another, forming attractive circular patterns.

ECHEVERIA 'LIPSTICK'

Echeveria agavoides

HARDINESS ZONE AND TEMPERATURE RANGE
9–11; 45°F–75°F

IDEAL LIGHTING
Full sun, partial sun

GROWING LOCATION
Outside is best; indoors must have bright sun. Not prone to **legginess** (see Glossary) like many other echeveria.

SIZE
6" tall; up to 12" wide

Mimics the appearance of an agave, with single-spine, pointy-tipped leaves. Easy to care for; makes lots of offsets. Gives nice flowers. Native to Mexico, Central America, and some parts of South America.

Special Features: Gorgeous green color, with thick, pointed leaves that get bright red on the edges (thus its name). It will get much redder depending on the amount of sun exposure; this is a great example of how a plant looks when **"stressed"** (see Glossary). It has pretty red flowers with yellow tips.

Care Instructions: Very easy; known to flower in all four seasons once established. It does not require much care: water outside during the very hot months of summer, water bimonthly inside and let dry in between waterings. Frequently used in **xeriscape** gardens (see Glossary).

Watch Out For: This is a drought-tolerant plant, with minimal pest issues. Look out for mealybugs and aphids; treat with a neem oil spray.

Arrangement Tips: Agavoides is a great plant for rock gardens and around larger companion plants, including other **clumping** succulents (see Glossary). It will send out lots of offsets and create a nice family of green and red plants that will pop against dark pebbles and black lava rock. It looks great in containers with smaller plants such as sedum planted in a border around it.

ECHEVERIA 'LOLA'

AKA HENS AND CHICKS

Echeveria 'Lola'

HARDINESS ZONE AND TEMPERATURE RANGE
9b-11; 45°F-80°F

IDEAL LIGHTING
Full sun to partial shade

GROWING LOCATION
Outdoors/indoors

SIZE
4-6" tall; 6-10" spread

Like all echeveria, Lola's ancestry is traced back to Mexico as a hybrid of *Echeveria lilacina* and *Echeveria derenbergii*. It features small light-green rosettes that grow in typical "hens and chicks" fashion, sending out babies that will form a mat of closely pressed-together plants in a planting bed. In spring and summer, it sends a short-stemmed coral-peach-yellow flower that hangs gently over the plant and is especially stunning when many bloom at once.

Special Features: Lola's coloring is remarkable. It looks like there is a pink light emanating from within the plant that sends a rosy glow just beneath the surface, giving its flesh an impressive illusion of depth.

Care Instructions: Water moderately in the summer and less during the colder winter months. Lola loves to be outdoors in direct sun in mild summer locations, but tends to sunburn, leaving ugly brown marks on its leaves in temperatures over 80°F. Unlike some succulents, whose papery dead bottom leaves provide protection for the rosette from water and decay, these dead leaves can serve as a nest for pests, so remove them immediately.

Watch Out For: Moths and caterpillars might chew holes in the leaves. Look for them on the underside of the leaves and discard them and their eggs. Treat the plant with a neem oil–based spray. Make sure your plant gets at least three to five hours of sun if it is living inside. Echeveria is prone to getting leggy without enough light: Its rosettes rise up high from the soil, searching for the sun. If the appearance bothers you, trim the head of the rosette, and after it callouses over replant it in fresh succulent soil.

Arrangement Tips: Plant in beds, where it will have room to spread and fill in with offsets. Great in container gardens with sedum and portulacaria, and lovely as a stand-alone plant in a decorative pot.

ESSENTIAL SUCCULENTS

MEXICAN FIRECRACKER

AKA FIRECRACKER PLANT, HENS AND CHICKS

Echeveria setosa

HARDINESS ZONE AND TEMPERATURE RANGE
9-11; 30°F-80°F

IDEAL LIGHTING
Full sun to partial sun

GROWING LOCATION
Outdoors/indoors

SIZE
3-5" tall; 24" spread

An explosion of bright-red flowers with yellow tips gives this unusual echeveria its nickname. The flowers can start in early spring and come in waves through fall. Native to Mexico, like all echeveria, setosa is a slow grower that may not get to full size for five years.

Special Features: This is one of an interesting subset of succulents that are covered in thick, short white hairs. It is said that the hairs of this fuzzy plant provide various protections to the plant, including insulation. Setosa is more cold-hardy than some other succulents, which may prove that theory.

Care Instructions: Though it is drought-tolerant, setosa actually likes regular water during the summer growth months. Water weekly, but don't let it sit in wet soil or a full water dish. During the winter dormant months, barely water at all.

Watch Out For: It is prone to mealybugs, vine weevil, and aphids. These bugs will kill your plant eventually if left alone, so check it regularly and treat accordingly.

Arrangement Tips: When in bloom, setosa will look great wherever it is: rock gardens, container gardens, or even hanging gardens. Pair with other fuzzy plants, like *Kalanchoe tomentosa,* for an interesting juxtaposition, or with semps, sedums, and delosperma for a floral feast for the eyes.

LAVENDER PEBBLES

AKA JEWEL LEAF PLANT, MOON ROCKS

Graptopetalum amethystinum

HARDINESS ZONE AND TEMPERATURE RANGE
9–11; 35°F–85°F

IDEAL LIGHTING
Full sun to partial sun;
likes some shade

GROWING LOCATION
Outdoors/indoors

SIZE
4-6" tall; 12-18" spread

The name Lavender Pebbles is quite accurate, as the leaves of this plant are plump and round and have a pink, violet, purple, and silver coloring. This Mexican native also has an interesting powdery coating on its leaves. It looks quite arresting when many plants grow together in a large clump, making it difficult to tell which leaf belongs to which rosette.

Special Features: Its spring blooms are star-shaped and yellow, with red triangles on the tips. The blooming may continue through summer and into fall.

Care Instructions: This plant is great outdoors in well-draining soil. In very hot regions it will require afternoon shade. Water moderately during the spring and summer, but keep the soil mostly dry during the cold months.

Watch Out For: This plant doesn't love the frost, as the leaves are so fat and full of water. Cover with frost cloth if it is outside during a surprise cold spell. Not known to be particularly attractive to pests, but always keep an eye out for mealybugs and aphids.

Arrangement Tips: Similar to the Opalina, the fantastic colors on this plant will complement many other bright succulents, such as *Sedum nussbaumerianum* and aeoniums like Zwartkop and Sunburst. Keep in a container inside, so you can more closely admire it. Use in a hanging basket; the spill can get to 18 inches long. It's also pretty in planting beds with chunky rocks.

OPALINA

Graptoveria 'Opalina'

HARDINESS ZONE AND TEMPERATURE RANGE
9b-11; down to 30°F

IDEAL LIGHTING
Partial sun

GROWING LOCATION
Outdoors/indoors

SIZE
6-8" tall; 4-6" wide

This plant reminds me of the coloring of the *Echeveria* 'Lola,' but with thicker, wider, and rounder leaves. It has whitish, blushing swirls of blues, greens, and purples in its leaves, which get pinker toward the edges and are more pronounced with bright direct sun. It was named for its similarity to the shifting colors of an opal. This plant is a hybrid of *Echeveria colorata* and *Graptopetalum amethystinum* (the previous plant on our list). Its parents are native to Mexico and the United States, and it was created in California.

 Special Features: Pretty blooms of yellow and orange will erupt on short stems in spring and summer.

Care Instructions: Water moderately, and never when the soil is still wet. The plant can grow leggy and tumble over a planter lip. Its stems will send out roots and connect itself to the soil as it moves along in nature. In a pot, it may become a hanging plant as it becomes top-heavy. You can leave it as is, or cut off the rosettes and repot them once the stems callous.

 Watch Out For: Root rot is a concern, so be careful when watering, especially during the winter months.

Arrangement Tips: Plant with tall branches of portulacaria above or next to green and blue echeverias. Plant with big pebbles in containers and in beds. Place where it will get a few hours of sun, but some shade, too, to prevent sunburn.

CHOCOLATE SOLDIER

AKA PANDA PLANT OR PUSSY EARS

Kalanchoe tomentosa

HARDINESS ZONE AND TEMPERATURE RANGE
9–12; down to 35°F

IDEAL LIGHTING
Full sun to partial sun;
very hot climates might
require some shade

GROWING LOCATION
Outdoors/indoors

SIZE
1–3' tall; 2–3' spread

When this Madagascar native blooms, it is thought to be a sign of wealth and prosperity for the owner. It is a great outdoor landscape plant, but will also live very happily indoors, as long as it receives bright light.

Special Features: This succulent features little hairs on its leaves and on its blooms, giving it a voluptuous, velvety look. Its new leaves are tannish-green and edged with a reddish tint to the tips, which will turn a deep mahogany when they mature. Its flowers are bell-shaped and also fuzzy; only outdoor plants will generally bloom.

Care Instructions: Chocolate Soldier, similar to many aeoniums, loves good ventilation, so if it is inside, make sure to keep it near a window. It also likes a bit more water in the summer. Propagate in the spring and summer by taking leaf or stem cuttings. If the leaves get dirty, use a paintbrush to gently clean them off, so as not to rub off the plant's hairs.

Watch Out For: This plant is very prone to water rot, so avoid watering the leaves if possible. It is also susceptible to rot when it is too cold, so keep it moderately warm in the wintertime. When transplanting, avoid jostling the plant's roots too much, as that may cause it to wilt right away.

Arrangement Tips: The plant's unique appearance makes it a crowd-pleaser wherever it lives. It looks terrific with almost any other succulents in a container garden. Pair it with Stonecrop Sedum and *Sempervivum* 'Red Robin' for a stylized array of color.

FLOWER DUST PLANT

Kalanchoe pumila

HARDINESS ZONE AND TEMPERATURE RANGE
9-11; down to 35°F

IDEAL LIGHTING
Full sun to partial sun

GROWING LOCATION
Outdoors/indoors

SIZE
Up to 8-12" tall, but generally
smaller; 2-3' spread

This is one of the smallest examples of the kalanchoe. Its silvery, purplish leaves are covered in slightly waxy white hairs, giving it a dusty look (thus its common name). It is a Madagascar native and really loves the heat, but like so many succulents, it is also adaptable to an indoor environment.

 Special Features: Gorgeous pink-violet flowers will cover this entire plant in late winter, continuing into the spring. Roundish leaves are marginally toothed with no spines. The leaves and flowers give a great color combination.

Care Instructions: Extremely drought-tolerant; acceptable for xeriscaping. Easy to propagate with leaf or stem cuttings. Cut off the dried flowers when they are done, and cut the plant back if the leaves look battered. This is a slow grower but will fill in nicely after being pruned.

Watch Out For: Virtually pest-free.

Arrangement Tips: If you live in a warm climate, this is an excellent outdoor plant. It's great in beds, containers, or to fill up any empty spaces. It's also a terrific border plant, as it will stay low and not overshadow medium-size plants, even when in full bloom. This is a fantastic indoor hanging plant, too; water moderately and allow to fully dry in between waterings.

AEONIUM 'KIWI'

Aeonium 'Kiwi'

HARDINESS ZONE AND TEMPERATURE RANGE
9–11; 30°F–75°F

IDEAL LIGHTING
Partial to full sun

GROWING LOCATION
Outdoors

SIZE
2–3' tall; 1–2' spread

Aeoniums are mostly native to Northern Africa. The Kiwi has thick, fleshy oval-shaped leaves with pointed tips. They tend to be yellowish–lime green in the center and get greener heading toward the bright pinkish-red edges.

Special Features: The coloration on the leaves will become more pronounced with sun exposure. It makes gorgeous yellow blooms in late spring or summer. It is a **monocarpic** plant (see Glossary), meaning it will flower once and then die. However, the rosettes may not bloom at the same time, and there is plenty of time to propagate this plant by stem cutting.

Care Instructions: Water regularly when first planting; change to occasional watering once established. In the summer, water just when there is very dry heat, and in the winter water monthly. Aeoniums will frequently be dormant in the summer and won't need much to drink during that time if the temperature is mild.

Watch Out For: Don't let this plant sit in water, as it is prone to root rot. It is also prone to sunburn and would prefer partial shade in a hotter climate. Sunburned leaves will turn brown and fall off. This won't kill the plant, but it won't look great until it grows new leaves.

Arrangement Tips: Looks great in rock gardens, as a specimen, with companions such as Blue Senecio, or with sedums such as Cape Blanco and Coppertone Stonecrop.

A Note About Aeoniums: While some people suggest aeoniums as a great indoor plant, my experience suggests they prefer to be outside, where they get a regular flow of air and feel the direct sunlight on their stems and branches. This contributes to the general health and elasticity of these plants.

ESSENTIAL SUCCULENTS

SUNBURST

AKA COPPER PINWHEEL

Aeonium 'Sunburst'

HARDINESS ZONE AND TEMPERATURE RANGE
9–11; 30°F–85°F

IDEAL LIGHTING
Full sun to partial shade

GROWING LOCATION
Outdoors

SIZE
1½–2' tall; 1½–2' wide

This showy aeonium has enormous rosettes that span up to 16 inches across, with a variety of different colors. The leaves can be bright yellow with varying thicknesses of green center striping, changing in size around each rosette. They can also be a creamier white with thick strips of variegated (**see Glossary**) green, like a brushstroke that hasn't been smoothed out, and pink coloring on the edges. Native to North Africa and the Canary Islands.

Special Features: This plant, like all aeoniums, is monocarpic, with white or yellow flower cones in spring, summer, and sometimes winter.

Care Instructions: This plant is drought-tolerant and can withstand very little water in the dormant summer if the weather is temperate.

Watch Out For: Curling of the leaves can suggest the plant is due for a good drink of water. Prone to sunburn in high heat.

Arrangement Tips: Sunburst looks great in rock gardens or containers. Plant it with Aeonium 'Zwartkop,' which has similar needs, or as a visual counterpoint to *Agave attenuata* 'Kara's Stripe' or Parry's Agave. It also looks dramatic with chunky lava rocks underneath an aloe tree.

BLACK ROSE

AKA BLACK BEAUTY, PURPLE CREST AEONIUM

Aeonium arboreum 'Zwartkop'

HARDINESS ZONE AND TEMPERATURE RANGE
9–11; 25°F–100°F

IDEAL LIGHTING
Full sun to partial shade

GROWING LOCATION
Outdoors

SIZE
1–6' tall; 2–3' spread

This aeonium has shiny, shiny 6- to 8-inch rosettes that are a waxy deep burgundy to black atop thin bare stems. All aeoniums are native to North Africa and the Canary Islands. This one will be darker and more striking in fuller sun and will have a green center with purplish leaves in full shade.

Special Features: Although this plant is monocarpic (it flowers, then dies), when it goes into bloom, it is an extraordinary display, sending a huge conical growth covered in hundreds of yellow flowers from the center of a single rosette. Flowers will last longer than a month and keep your attention the entire time. The branch that blooms will die, but the plant may have many branches that bloom at different times or during different years.

Care Instructions: Like the Kiwi, Zwartkop goes mostly dormant in the summer. It likes moderate water during the winter growing months and can take a bit more heat than its other aeonium family members.

Watch Out For: Sometimes it will drop leaves during the dormant months, as it focuses its energy on its stems and roots. Water monthly during this time to keep it fully hydrated. Keep an eye out for mealybugs and spider mites. This plant is said to be deer-resistant.

Arrangement Tips: Great as a **specimen plant** (see Glossary). Terrific in containers with cactus and sedum, or as a stand-alone plant. Contrast it with *Echeveria imbricata* and *Sedum* 'Red Robin,' or go all in with dark plants like *Echeveria* 'Black Prince,' *Sedum spathulifolium* 'Purpureum' and *Sedum* 'Vera Jameson.'

PIG'S EAR

AKA RED EDGE PIG'S EAR

Cotyledon orbiculata

HARDINESS ZONE AND TEMPERATURE RANGE
6-11b; down to 25°F

IDEAL LIGHTING
Full sun

GROWING LOCATION
Outdoors/indoors

SIZE
6-8" tall; 10-12" spread

Cotyledon orbiculata has whitish-silvery leaves with a thin red line around its perimeter. It is a native of South Africa, where it has been used medicinally to treat warts, corns, inflammation, and even epilepsy. Its leaves are covered in a powdery dust that helps insulate the plant from extreme brightness and drought.

Special Features: From summer to fall, this shrub sends tall flower stems high above itself. Each has 10 to 20 long, asymmetrical buds that open into glorious bell-shaped flowers with silky petals turned up at the ends to show off the stamen within. This is my personal favorite of all succulent flowers.

Care Instructions: While desiring full sun, Cotyledon will tolerate partial shade. It also is a bit standoffish, generally wanting some space around itself for ventilation, which helps prevent diseases like root rot.

Watch Out For: Not many pests attack this plant, but look out for slugs and snails, and apply copper tape if the plant is in a pot that can be circled with it. Otherwise, apply pesticides.

Arrangement Tips: Pig's Ear is lovely in rock gardens and in beds with aeoniums and agaves. Also makes a great feature in its own planter, where it will delight you with its warm-weather flowers.

BLUE CHALK STICKS

AKA BLUE SENECIO
Senecio mandraliscae

HARDINESS ZONE AND TEMPERATURE RANGE
9-11: down to 15°F-20°F

IDEAL LIGHTING
Full sun to partial sun

GROWING LOCATION
Outdoors

SIZE
1-2' tall; 2-3' spread

Silvery blue leaves shaped like fingers curving up toward the sky grow from thick, ropy stems crawling across the ground, with small white flowers blooming in the summer. Native to South Africa.

Special Features: Blue Senecio, like many sedums and other ground cover succulents, grows tightly together, with its roots mingling to form a dense mat underneath the soil. Its bright-blue leaves are coated with a dusty, chalky powder.

Care Instructions: This plant is a winter grower, like aeoniums, with dormancy during the summer. Although it is drought-tolerant, it will grow much faster with steady irrigation.

Watch Out For: Mealybugs, aphids, and spider mites like to eat this plant. Stay on it, especially during the dormant summer months. Remove dead flowers, and trim stalks regularly for appearance. Cut entire plant way back every few years to avoid long leggy stems.

Arrangement Tips: Looks great as a border plant in rock gardens and containers. The bright color complements burgundy aeoniums, orange sedums, and other bright-colored succulents. Will dangle over a container and then curve back upward, which looks especially pretty while flowering.

FISHHOOKS SENECIO

AKA STRING OF BANANAS, NECKLACE PLANT

Senecio radicans

HARDINESS ZONE AND TEMPERATURE RANGE
9–11; 25°F–100°F

IDEAL LIGHTING
Full sun to light shade

GROWING LOCATION
Indoors/outdoors

SIZE
3–5" high, with dangling stems that can reach 4' long

Native to South Africa, this plant got its name from its unusually shaped leaves that can look like hooks or bright-green bananas. They line up in single file along stems that will grow very long.

Special Features: Its tiny flowers, shaped like little puffballs, have the unusual quality in the succulent world of having a lovely fragrance, much like cinnamon. Another senecio, the String of Pearls, has a similar flower with a similar smell.

Care Instructions: Outside, it needs bright shade if it is in a hot region. Inside, it is a very easy plant to grow with plenty of bright light. Give it a lot of water during the warm months, always allowing the soil to dry in between waterings. Neglect it a bit during the cooler winter. This plant is easy to propagate from stem cuttings, so whenever it needs a trim, replant the cuttings and pass along the new plants to your friends.

Watch Out For: It doesn't get attacked by many pests, though I've seen mealybugs on them in California. Treat accordingly.

Arrangement Tips: Radicans are great alone or with companions in a hanging basket. Also a great container plant as either a feature or one of the pack. It will act as a ground cover if you let it, crawling up the soil and rooting along the way, so it's great between rocks and pavers where you won't step on it.

VERTICAL LEAF SENECIO

AKA LAVENDER STEPS, LAVENDER LIPS

Senecio crassissimus

HARDINESS ZONE AND TEMPERATURE RANGE
9b-11; down to 30°F

IDEAL LIGHTING
Full sun to partial sun

GROWING LOCATION
Outdoors/indoors

SIZE
24" tall; 18" wide

Quite different from most senecios, which are usually characterized by flexible stems and dangling foliage, crassissimus has stiff, upright purple stems with flat, glossy upturned leaves that are greenish-blue and decorated with purple edges. The leaves' interesting orientation means that when the sun is at its hottest, only a small portion of each leaf faces that heat, which protects the plant from burn and intensifies its coloring. It is native to Madagascar.

Special Features: Blossoming off a long stem, its winter flowers are bright yellow and shaped like daisies.

Care Instructions: When it reaches maximum height, which it can do in just a few seasons, it has a tendency to get floppy on top. In the spring, prune about 6 to 8 inches to control it; plant the cuttings after their stems scab. Make sure this plant has excellent drainage in sandy soil, which will benefit from an annual fertilizer for nutrients.

Watch Out For: Similar to other senecios, this plant has few pests. Look out for scale and mealybugs and treat accordingly.

Arrangement Tips: The purple foliage is showy, making this a great plant in a colorful garden bed. Looks fantastic with sempervivum, aloes, sedums, and echeverias. Plant solo in a container for an eye-catching indoor or porch plant. Since it is humidity-tolerant, it is suitable for a **terrarium** (see Glossary), but it needs to be a large one or the plant will outgrow the vessel in a year or so.

THE 50 BEST SUCCULENT VARIETIES FOR BEGINNERS *33*

JADE

Crassula ovata

HARDINESS ZONE AND TEMPERATURE RANGE
9–11; ideal temperature is 65°F–75°F during the day and 45°F–60°F at night.

IDEAL LIGHTING
Full sun, partial sun

GROWING LOCATION
Outdoors/indoors, with as much sun as possible indoors.

SIZE
Outside can grow to nearly 10' tall and spread wide and bushy, up to 6'. Inside, it grows shorter and less bushy.

Wonderful low-maintenance landscape plant with a firework display of flowers exploding from each clump of leaves. Native to South Africa and Mozambique.

Special Features: Tiny, ornate flowers and leaves that are susceptible to stressing in the most beautiful way, with leaves turning bright red as a result. This long-lasting plant makes a great gift that can endure beyond a human lifetime. It is also said to bring good luck and is one of a few with the nickname "money tree."

Care Instructions: Very easy to care for, with nearly no needs outside and only needing somewhat regular bimonthly waterings inside. It doesn't want to get too dry inside and will drop leaves to let you know it is not drinking enough. You can snap off its rubbery branches and easily replant them directly into soil. Unlike many succulents, this can be rooted in water, which makes it a nice plant to have in a bud vase on a dining room or coffee table.

Watch Out For: Susceptible to mealybugs and powdery mildew, which will look like powdered sugar. Use sulfur or a neem oil–based spray to treat the powdery mildew. You may also need to remove some of the leaves if you catch the mildew late and it is very heavy.

Arrangement Tips: Can be an ornamental ("specimen") plant in the garden, growing to both tree shape and size. In cold climates it is generally grown indoors, where it will grow longer, thinner branches and spread out widely. Because of its interesting treelike shape, it can be a compelling container and terrarium plant, mimicking a bonsai tree.

SILVER DOLLAR JADE

Crassula arborescens

HARDINESS ZONE AND TEMPERATURE RANGE
9–11; 25°F–75°F

IDEAL LIGHTING
Full sun, partial sun

GROWING LOCATION
Outdoors/indoors;
prefers outdoor

SIZE
Can grow into a small bush/
tree up to 4' tall and 3' wide if
planted in the ground; will stay
small in a smaller container.

Similar in size to a silver dollar, this crassula grows similarly to the Ovata, with large, thick branches that will grow easily with little or no attention once established. It has gorgeous bronze foliage with silvery-white round leaves faintly polka-dotted with red marks and a reddish stripe around the perimeter of the leaf. Native to the Eastern and Western Capes of South Africa.

Special Features: Pretty star-shaped white flowers will emerge as it blooms.

Care Instructions: Plant in soil that drains well. Once established, perfect for xeriscape gardens. Propagates very easily using stem cuttings.

Watch Out For: This plant can get quite heavy in its leaves and branches. If you want it to get tall, prune it liberally so that it doesn't hang over. Are you sure you have a Silver Dollar Jade? This plant looks quite a bit like the *Cotyledon orbiculata*. How can you be sure which you have? The flowers are completely different and will tell the tale.

Arrangement Tips: Similar to the conventional jade, this plant will be a great specimen in a garden, pulling attention to its interesting color. Set a big rock in front of it, and plant Stonecrop Sedum around that. The yellows and oranges of the sedum will contrast beautifully with the silvery leaves of this crassula.

CRASSULA 'CALICO KITTEN'
Crassula pellucida subsp. marginalis 'Variegata'

HARDINESS ZONE AND TEMPERATURE RANGE
9–11; 55°F–75°F

IDEAL LIGHTING
Full sun, partial sun, filtered sun, light shade

GROWING LOCATION
Outdoors/indoors

SIZE
2–4" tall, long trailing stems up to 12" long; will clump and spread out even farther if allowed.

This is a great clumping plant with stunning shades of purple, red, cream, and green on its small, stacked heart-shaped leaves. It will spread nicely and become a gorgeous and unusual ground cover. Native to the Eastern Cape of South Africa.

Special Features: Can turn reddish-purple when stressed. Will send out lovely little white firework flowers above the plant that will call attention to the brightness of its leaves.

Care Instructions: Once established, it needs very little attention; trim the flowers once they have dried. Propagates very simply with leaf and stem cuttings.

Watch Out For: Prone to mealybugs and fungal issues. Keep it dry; don't overwater. Never let it sit in water, and if it is in a container with a dish, always empty the dish a few minutes after watering. Leaves are fragile, so handle as little as possible. Sensitive to frost; keep warm.

Arrangement Tips: Clumps beautifully; looks great in hanging containers that show off its explosive white flowers blooming intermittently throughout the year. The blooms are thought to attract bees and butterflies. Drape over shiny rocks in terrariums for an elegant look.

STRING OF BUTTONS

Crassula perforata

HARDINESS ZONE AND TEMPERATURE RANGE
9–11; 45°F–75°F

IDEAL LIGHTING
Full sun, partial sun; in very hot climates will require some afternoon shade

GROWING LOCATION
Outdoors/indoors

SIZE
1–2' tall; 2–3' wide

Crassulas are easy to grow and propagate and are very forgiving indoors or outside. Native to South Africa. Good in the ground, in containers, or even as a hanging plant.

 Special Features: The greenish, silvery leaves in many crassulas are geometrically shaped and stacked on top of each other. They have pinkish edges, which will become more pronounced with full sun. The perforata sends out pretty little yellow flowers at the top that highlight the range of colors on this plant.

Care Instructions: This plant can take care of itself very well and doesn't need much water. Simple to propagate with offsets, stem cuttings, and leaves. Use stem cuttings high on the stalks that are less woody than the older stems below. Very drought-tolerant. Used frequently in xeriscape landscapes

Watch Out For: Low risk of pests, but watch out for mealybugs and aphids inside.

Arrangement Tips: Will do great indoors as a companion to your haworthia or aloe. Also nice outside among Blue Senecio and around larger agave. Will give nice height to smaller terrarium plantings, towering over sedum and smaller echeveria.

ELEPHANT FOOD

AKA ELEPHANT BUSH, PORKBUSH, DWARF JADE PLANT

Portulacaria afra

HARDINESS ZONE AND TEMPERATURE RANGE
9a–11b; down to 25–30°F

IDEAL LIGHTING
Full sun to full shade

GROWING LOCATION
Outdoors/indoors

SIZE
8–15' tall; 4–6' spread

Little roundish green leaves populate thin, brittle, reddish branches on this South African native. It's not related to jade, but bears a superficial resemblance, giving it the "dwarf" nickname. Tiny star-shaped pink flowers appear at the ends of the branches, only to give way to semitranslucent berries in the summer, though rarely when planted inside.

Special Features: Eaten by some humans and a lot of wildlife, this succulent's plump little leaves provide a sour tang to soups, salads, and meats. It also has strong carbon-cleaning capabilities and is known to clean the air more than other plants.

Care Instructions: This plant demands bright light and well-draining soil. Intense sun can stress the plant, turning its tips a pleasing red. But it can also cause sunburn to the leaves, so striking the right balance might be challenging.

Watch Out For: Very few pests attack this plant. Be careful not to overwater, and scan for mealybugs often.

Arrangement Tips: This plant grows naturally in rocky outcrops and sloping mountainsides, so it is a natural for rock gardens and gritty soil. In colder climates, it fills a hanging planter gloriously, with its branches spreading up and down. Because of its treelike appearance, it looks great hanging over smaller plants and fulfills the same role in open terrariums with other drought-tolerant plants.

RED APPLE
Aptenia cordifolia

HARDINESS ZONE AND TEMPERATURE RANGE
9-12; 40°F-80°F

IDEAL LIGHTING
Full sun, partial sun

GROWING LOCATION
Outdoors/indoors

SIZE
1-3" tall; 18-24" spread

Aptenia has fleshy green, heart- and oval-shaped leaves with a fast-growing root system that fans out to form a carpet of ground cover. Native to Southern Africa.

Special Features: Explodes with daisylike flowers bursting throughout the plant in either pink, red, purple, yellow, or white. The flowers open during the bright hours and close at night. In some areas, it is used medicinally as an anti-inflammatory, poultice, and deodorant. It's also known as a love charm.

Care Instructions: Water when dry only. No need for fertilizer, as this plant will grow strongly even if never watered. Trim for shape as needed or desired using sharp pruners. Can be immediately replanted in other beds or containers. If in a container, bring it inside when the temperature drops below 40°F.

Watch Out For: Prone to root rot, so plant in gritty, very well-draining soil. Water very lightly if at all in the winter. Aptenia has a tendency to climb around other plants, so if you plant it near trees, keep it trimmed around the base. Weed regularly.

Arrangement Tips: With its sparkling flowers, this is lovely ground cover. Also great for soil erosion control on a hill or slope. Terrific in tree wells and along paths.

SAND ROSE

Anacampseros rufescens

HARDINESS ZONE AND TEMPERATURE RANGE
10-11; down to 25°F

IDEAL LIGHTING
Full sun, partial shade

GROWING LOCATION
Outdoors/indoors

SIZE
3-4" tall; 4-6" spread

Native to Southern Africa, this small clumping plant can get lush colors in full sun. Its botanical name is very old and has been used to describe different plants for hundreds of years, including herbs used to lure lost love homeward. It flowers in the spring, but unless it is a bright, sunny day of at least 85°F, the long maroon buds probably won't open. The flowers can be pink, purple, or violet.

 Special Features: The leaves are triangular, with green on most tops and pinks and purples on the bottom. The leaves are spaced close together on the stems, and the plant appears a little jiggly as it flops one way or the other. There are delicate hairs all over the stems and leaves of this plant.

Care Instructions: Very easy to propagate from seed. Water only when dry. Bring this drought-tolerant plant inside in cold climates; it will die from frost.

Watch Out For: Mealybugs, aphids. Treat accordingly.

Arrangement Tips: Its interesting coloring makes this plant a favorite in container gardens, next to a small sedum or with *Senecio* 'Fishhooks' crawling across the soil around it. Place all that in front of a tall aenonium for a vibrant display.

PIXIE LIME

AKA TEARDROP

Peperomia orba

HARDINESS ZONE AND TEMPERATURE RANGE
10–11; 50°F–85°F

IDEAL LIGHTING
Partial sun, partial shade;
won't tolerate low light

GROWING LOCATION
Outdoors/indoors

SIZE
3–4" tall; 3–5" wide

This dwarf cultivar is native to Central and South America, where it grows under the dappled light of the canopy in the rain forest. There it grows epiphytically (living on other plants; see Glossary), with very little or no soil, on tree trunks and branches with air plants.

Special Features: This one breaks the rule: It is unusual in that it prefers higher humidity and more water than most succulent plants, and as a result is a fantastic houseplant in most climates.

Care Instructions: The Pixie Lime wants moist soil. Water weekly, but don't leave it sitting in water in a dish. In very hot climates, mist the leaves during summer, but not in winter. In warm regions, it can be grown outdoors as a ground cover in partial shade.

Watch Out For: Don't expect fast growth; this plant will stay small. It thrives tight in its little pot, so repot for fresh soil, but don't worry about planting up for growth. Though rare, it might get a virus called ring spot, which will result in distorted foliage and rings on the leaves. Destroy those plants and start again.

Arrangement Tips: Nice on its own in an indoor window planter, or in a hanging planter where its stems and leaves will dangle. Also great in a wet terrarium, with African violets and other high-humidity, water-loving plants.

ESSENTIAL SUCCULENTS

LOBSTER FLOWER

AKA BLUE COLEUS

Plectranthus neochilus

HARDINESS ZONE AND TEMPERATURE RANGE
9-11; down to 25-30°F

IDEAL LIGHTING
Full sun to bright shade

GROWING LOCATION
Outdoors

SIZE
1-2' tall; very wide spread

A skunky aroma reminiscent of marijuana emanates from the neochilus, which some people will love. The grayish-green leaves are pointed, notched, and very soft. It grows faster than many succulents and will fill a planting bed in little over one season. It's native to Southern Africa.

Special Features: The blooms of this plant are 3 to 6 inches tall, deep purple, very fragrant, and might come during any of the four seasons, but can be expected from spring to late fall.

Care Instructions: This is a great plant for dry locations. It doesn't need much water and will be happy only receiving winter rains. After the blooms dry, prune this plant back for appearance. This is one of the easiest succulents to propagate, so prune regularly to maintain shape and location.

Watch Out For: This plant is not known to be attacked by many pests; in fact, its fragrance is thought to make it repellent to deer, snails, and even snakes. The leaves will wilt when it is very thirsty, so give them a drink if you see this.

Arrangement Tips: This is a great ground cover and will look luscious when in bloom. It's lovely in hanging baskets, containers, and rock gardens. It is used for erosion control on the sides of hills because it will hold the dirt in place under its dense root system. It is a great shade plant in very hot tropical areas, and a fantastic, sunny xeriscape plant in moderate temperatures with rainy winters.

HARDY ICE PLANT

Delosperma cooperi

HARDINESS ZONE AND TEMPERATURE RANGE
6-10: in dry zones hardy
down to -20°F

IDEAL LIGHTING
Full sun

GROWING LOCATION
Outdoors/indoors

SIZE
3-6" tall; 24" spread

This noninvasive ice plant is native to Southern Africa. It has fleshy little green leaves and is extremely hardy, making it a great outdoor plant in colder areas.

Special Features: It is known for its gorgeous, daisylike magenta flowers that can carpet bloom during the warm season. The 2-inch-wide blooms make this plant a prized ornamental.

Care Instructions: It is drought-tolerant and salt-tolerant, so it can be planted near the sea. Water regularly during the first year it is planted outside, then much less to allow it to harden off to cold nights and less care. Water a bit more when planted in containers.

Watch Out For: Must have well-draining soil and/or pots or will grow poorly and possibly die. A bit prone to aphids and mealybugs; treat accordingly.

Arrangement Tips: Plant as a spectacular ground cover on the sides of hills, or in rock gardens as an accent. Fill a container for a stunning bloom and prune as needed. Plant with sedums and sempervivums for color variety.

DANCING BONES CACTUS

AKA DRUNKARD'S DREAM, SPICE CACTUS, BOTTLE CACTUS

Hatiora salicornioides, aka Rhipsalis salicornioides

HARDINESS ZONE AND TEMPERATURE RANGE
10-12; down to 25°F–30°F

IDEAL LIGHTING
Light shade to full sun

GROWING LOCATION
Outdoors/indoors

SIZE
12-18" tall; 12-18" spread

Small and bushy, Dancing Bones Cactus is native to Brazil, where it grows epiphytically in dappled sunlight below the canopy of the rain forest. It is mostly spineless, but an older plant may develop spiny growth around its base. It is made up of little sections of bottle- or sausage-shaped foliage connected to each other in segments.

Special Features: Its small, bell-shaped flowers of deep orange and yellow pop out of slender branches and eventually give way to translucent reddish berries.

Care Instructions: Give this plant indirect bright light and feed it regularly with water and fertilizer during its spring and summer growing months. Water only occasionally and do not fertilize during its winter dormancy. Propagate simply by breaking off the little branches and replanting them in soil.

Watch Out For: Very few pests will hurt this plant; avoid direct sun and overwatering.

Arrangement Tips: Because this plant is humidity-tolerant, it is an excellent choice for terrariums with cactus, gasteria, and sedum. Will also look great in hanging baskets and container gardens. Can be pruned for shape.

DONKEY'S TAIL

AKA BURRO'S TAIL, BURRITO

Sedum morganianum

HARDINESS ZONE AND TEMPERATURE RANGE
10–11; 40°F–80°F

IDEAL LIGHTING
Full sun, partial shade

GROWING LOCATION
Outdoors/indoors; doesn't
like extreme heat or cold.

SIZE
Trailing branches can
reach 24" long

Features overlapping droplet-shaped, silvery light-green leaves covering long stems. Native to Mexico; most likely to bloom if left outside.

Special Features: Flowers emerge from the very tips of the branches, opening up into fascinating star shapes of red, white, and violet blooms. Blooms are best enjoyed if the plant is up high, as they will face downward at the end of the stem.

Care Instructions: Water moderately when the soil is dry during the active months, March to September. Morganianum is susceptible to root rot, so make sure you have great drainage, and don't overwater, especially during the dormant winter months when it needs about half the attention it gets the rest of the year. Propagates easily with stem or leaf cuttings. The leaves will live for a very long time when removed and generally will push out roots in just a few days.

Watch Out For: The leaves of this plant will pop off very easily when handled, so get it into a great place to live and then leave it alone as much as possible. Repot rarely and change the soil when you do. Aphids and mealybugs are the main pest concerns. Either spray down with a low-alcohol mix (5:1 ratio of water to alcohol) or a neem oil–based mix to mitigate.

Arrangement Tips: This is a great hanging plant. Put it in a sunny spot where it won't be jostled by passersby.

PORK AND BEANS

Sedum x rubrotinctum 'Stonecrop'

HARDINESS ZONE AND TEMPERATURE RANGE
9–11; 50°F–75°F

IDEAL LIGHTING
Full sun, partial sun

GROWING LOCATION
Outdoors/indoors

SIZE
Up to 12" high; 8–12" spread. Sends out roots along the stem and will spread out nicely as a ground cover.

Showy and colorful; will stress nicely. Comes in pinks, reds, greens, and yellows; tips can get bright in the summer and become greener in the winter. Native to Mexico.

Special Features: Pretty yellow flowers in late winter; can withstand some colder weather, but mostly thought of as a tender plant that should avoid overwatering and extreme weather conditions.

Care Instructions: Drought-tolerant; can be mostly left alone. Should not be handled often, as the leaves will separate from the stems quite easily. Some people get a mild irritation from the sap of this plant, and it is not advised to ingest it, as it can lead to a stomachache.

Watch Out For: This plant is not known to be tasty to most pests; however, it can rot easily if it is overwatered and not allowed to dry out in between waterings. Direct sun during the winter can be detrimental to its health as well.

Arrangement Tips: Great for rock gardens; its architectural form provides height in container gardens. In outdoor gardens it will stay close to the ground around taller plants like *Graptoveria* 'Fred Ives,' agaves, and aloes. The bright, colorful leaves will contrast nicely with greener plants.

CAPE BLANCO STONECROP

Sedum spathulifolium 'Cape Blanco'

HARDINESS ZONE AND TEMPERATURE RANGE
5-9; can withstand
cold down to -10°F

IDEAL LIGHTING
Full sun, partial sun

GROWING LOCATION
Outdoors/indoors

SIZE
2-6" tall with a 24" spread

Features tiny rosettes of a silvery-green color, sometimes tinged with purple. Native to Oregon and grown widely along the Northwestern coast. One of many sedums with the Stonecrop nickname, it is rumored to have this name because only stones need less attention and live longer.

Special Features: It will send out clusters of starry yellow flowers in the early summer. There is a hybrid version called "purpureum" that is deep purple with similar flowers and growing conditions. Some people eat it raw in salads, soups, and stir-fries. Harvest in the morning before it becomes more acidic. Consuming more than a handful of leaves can cause an upset stomach.

Care Instructions: When first planted, water weekly to help roots establish. Afterward, it can be left alone with little or no irrigation. Needs great drainage to thrive.

Watch Out For: Wet areas with bad drainage will cause this plant to die back. Very few pests are known to attack it, and because it is drought- and deer-resistant, it's a desirable landscape plant.

Arrangement Tips: Plant along rock walls, on the edges of paths, and around larger specimen plants such as agave and aeonium. Its shape and color will highlight the greens in its companion plants. Great in dry terrariums planted with cactus and watered very infrequently.

CORSICAN STONECROP

AKA BLUE TEARS SEDUM, LOVE & TANGLES

Sedum dasyphyllum 'Major'

HARDINESS ZONE AND TEMPERATURE RANGE
7a-10b; -10°F-80°F

IDEAL LIGHTING
Full sun

GROWING LOCATION
Outdoors/indoors

SIZE
3-5" tall; 12" spread

Miniature clusters of foliage (though bigger than the 'Minor' version) with grapelike blue, green, and purple leaves. Will create a tight carpet as a ground cover, and the leaves will turn more purple in hot sun. Native to the Mediterranean region of Europe. Typically found in its natural habitat growing between and among volcanic rocks.

Special Features: Fantastic cold-region ground cover. Dasyphyllum will deal with extreme temperatures in both directions. In spring and summer, this sedum will send out pink buds that will open into pretty white flowers.

Care Instructions: Very adaptable to a variety of planting locations. Can handle conditions many other plants do not like, such as very hot sun and very little water. Broken leaves will re-root where they fall, helping it spread nicely into whatever area you let it. Super easy to propagate with divisions and also with leaves. Just replant divisions immediately, set leaves on soil, and leave them alone.

Watch Out For: Very few known pests, but, like most succulents, this plant is susceptible to root rot.

Arrangement Tips: Great for rock walls, containers, between stepping-stones, and in beds around larger plants. Gives great texture and context to various-sized companion plants. Terrific in dry terrariums with haworthia, gasteria, and cactus.

COPPERTONE STONECROP

AKA GOLDEN SEDUM, SEDUM STONECROP
Sedum nussbaumerianum

HARDINESS ZONE AND TEMPERATURE RANGE
9–11; down to 30°F

IDEAL LIGHTING
Full sun to partial sun

GROWING LOCATION
Outdoors/indoors

SIZE
4–7" tall; 2–3' spread

This plant has very large leaves for a sedum. Thick, pointy blades form 2- to 3-inch-wide rosettes. Flowers in winter through spring with mildly fragrant small white blooms. Native to Mexico.

 Special Features: Coppertone has incredible color. At its dullest, it is a rusty tan with reddish pigments just below the surface. Add heat and reduce water, and the color turns vivid orange with bright red and apricot hues glowing almost translucently in the sun.

Care Instructions: Plant in very well-draining medium. Water moderately in the summer and much less in the winter. Can be neglected in all seasons. It tends to grow leggy in both great sun and partial sun, and can eventually be cut back and the heads replanted when they are at maximum height.

Watch Out For: Very few pests, but don't overwater; its color will suffer, and root rot is always a concern.

Arrangement Tips: Coppertone's bright coloring makes you want to pair it with other vibrantly colored plants like Blue Senecio, *Aeonium* 'Kiwi,' and *Agave* 'Blue Glow.' It's fantastic in rock gardens and containers as fill, lovely in hanging baskets by itself, and stunning against rocks and boulders of any size.

ESSENTIAL SUCCULENTS

SNAKE PLANT

AKA MOTHER-IN-LAW'S TONGUE

Sansevieria trifasciata

HARDINESS ZONE AND TEMPERATURE RANGE
9–11; 40°F–80°F

IDEAL LIGHTING
Partial sun to full sun

GROWING LOCATION
Outdoors/indoors

SIZE
25–60" tall; 2" wide leaves

Sansevieria is native to Angola, Africa. It sends out leaves from rhizomes (a type of stem that can function like a root) under the soil. The tall leaves of the Snake Plant are wide, like thick blades of swordlike grass edged in gray, silver, gold, yellow, and green.

Special Features: With enough light, this plant will produce a 1- to 3-foot-long spike of aromatic white flowers edged in pink. It may bloom less than once in 10 years when living indoors.

Care Instructions: This incredibly easy-to-care-for plant is a favorite for offices and public buildings. Indoors, it requires a well-draining pot and will acclimate to a wide range of light, from full to very little sun. It can survive a lot of neglect, including being root-bound or water-deprived. Water every three weeks at the most during its warm growing seasons and much less during the winter. Feel free to wipe the leaves with a moist cloth to keep them free of dust.

Watch Out For: Drainage is the most important thing to keep an eye on, as this plant is prone to indoor attack by spider mites, mealybugs, and aphids. Treat accordingly.

Arrangement Tips: This plant looks fabulous in multiples in large containers. Use preserved moss like Spanish moss or sphagnum as a topdressing. Plant outdoors in warm climates as a back border to a garden bed. Indoors, use with other neglectable plants, like gasteria, haworthia, and cactus.

CYLINDRICAL SNAKE PLANT

AKA AFRICAN SPEAR, ELEPHANT'S TOOTHPICK

Sansevieria cylindrica

HARDINESS ZONE AND TEMPERATURE RANGE
9–11; 55°F–80°F

IDEAL LIGHTING
Partial sun to full sun

GROWING LOCATION
Outdoors/indoors

SIZE
12"–84" tall; spreads as much as you let it

The Cylindrical Snake Plant is native to Angola, Africa. It sends out leaves from rhizomes (a type of stem that can function like a root) under the soil. The leaves are about 1 inch thick and consist of tightly banded spikes of green, with slight variegation coming to a point at the top.

Special Features: The leaves will grow in a fan shape but are frequently sold in pots with a few propagated spears standing next to each other, and even sometimes braided together. With enough light, this plant will produce a foot-long spike of aromatic white flowers edged in pink.

Care Instructions: Sansevieria is the ultimate neglect plant. Give it succulent soil and a well-draining pot and you can mostly leave it alone. Water monthly during the warm months and every other month during the winter. Keep the leaves dust-free with a moist cloth.

Watch Out For: A leaf will essentially stop growing if its point gets broken, so be careful with the tips of this plant. It may also stop growing with insufficient light, but chances are good it will still stay alive.

Arrangement Tips: This is a great container plant. Use by itself or with Fishhooks Senecio or another plant that will spill over the edges to provide depth to your arrangement.

HOUSELEEK

AKA HENS AND CHICKS

Sempervivum tectorum

HARDINESS ZONE AND TEMPERATURE RANGE
5-10; down to -20°F

IDEAL LIGHTING
Full sun

GROWING LOCATION
Outdoors/indoors

SIZE
4-6" tall; 6-24" spread

Sempervivum is a Latin term meaning "always living." This plant earns its name by sending out tons of babies (offsets) to ensure its never-ending life. The individual rosettes will bloom spectacularly and then die (they are monocarpic). However, there will be so many rosettes that another will easily take its place. Tectorum, a common varietal of this European native, has blue-green leaves in a tight rosette with purplish-reddish highlights toward the edges.

Special Features: The one-time-only bloom is stunning, with a thick yet soft stem extending up from the rosette and opening into an intricate array of star-shaped bright-pink flowers. Know that though this plant is going to die, it will leave you with a happy heart. Historically, semps were once planted on thatched roofs as a fire retardant. This is yet another reason to install a living (green) roof.

Care Instructions: Plant in well-draining soil; water moderately. Keep dry in winter. Remove dead flowers and rosettes.

Watch Out For: Susceptible to crown rot but will dry some bottom leaves in an attempt to protect itself from excess moisture. Also susceptible to endophyllum rust, an orangish fungus that will grow on the leaves of plants. Remove those leaves and treat the plant with a fungicide, like neem oil, until all signs of the rust are gone.

Arrangement Tips: Plant in rock gardens, directly in rock walls, along paths, in tree wells, in container gardens, in vertical gardens, and as a companion to echeveria, sedum, and other full-sun succulents.

COBWEB SEMPERVIVUM

AKA HENS AND CHICKS

Sempervivum arachnoideum

HARDINESS ZONE AND TEMPERATURE RANGE
5-8; down to -25°F

IDEAL LIGHTING
Full sun to partial shade

GROWING LOCATION
Outdoors/indoors

SIZE
2-4" tall; 8-10" spread

Tight rosettes of green leaves covered in webbing reminiscent of a spider's web characterize this cold-hardy succulent. Frequently mistaken for an actual spiderweb, this natural fiber protects the plant from real bugs, insulates it from the cold, and can shield it from other weather conditions such as wind and hot sun. All sempervivums are native to the mountains of Europe.

Special Features: Like all semps, it features a truly spectacular bloom. The onetime-only bloom is stunning, with a thick yet soft stem extending up from the rosette and opening into an intricate array of star-shaped bright-pink flowers.

Care Instructions: Keep it dry during the cold winter. If indoors, make sure it has plenty of light. Cut off and discard dead plant matter.

Watch Out For: Not known for pests. Always keep it from sitting in wet soil. Keep it in a well-draining pot. Provide it with some shade if it is getting a lot of hot direct sunlight.

Arrangement Tips: Plant in rock gardens, directly in rock walls, along paths, in tree wells, in container gardens, in vertical gardens, and as a companion to echeveria, sedum, and other full-sun succulents.

QUEEN OF THE NIGHT

AKA DUTCHMAN'S PIPE CACTUS, NIGHT-BLOOMING CEREUS

Epiphyllum oxypetalum

HARDINESS ZONE AND TEMPERATURE RANGE
10-11; down to 50°F

IDEAL LIGHTING
Bright filtered light

GROWING LOCATION
Outdoors/indoors

SIZE
8'-10' tall

Not actually in the Cereus family, this Central American native has its nickname because it generally only blooms at night and each bloom lasts for only one or two nights. The long, notched, waxy leaves are on flattened stems that won't grow upward without support. Because the foliage is bright green and propagates very easily, you will sometimes see vendors selling individual leaves with the name and flower type written in marker on the leaf.

Special Features: The flower buds grow very long, 7 to 10 inches, and will finally open just briefly in the middle of the night. The fragrance is intoxicating, especially if a batch of buds all open at once. It can have many crops of flowers over the course of one season. The buds are pink and the flowers are a silky white.

Care Instructions: This plant wants moderate water, only when dry. During summer it likes a bit of humidity. Cold weather during the drier winter months will encourage summer blooms.

Watch Out For: Mealybugs, aphids, and spider mites might try to make a home in your plant. It is prone to root rot, especially in the winter. Water it sparingly during those months.

Arrangement Tips: Great in a hanging basket. Will grow upward with stakes. Can be trained to grow up and around windows. Plant it with flowering cactus for a nice juxtaposition.

ZEBRA PLANT

Haworthia fasciata or Haworthiopsis fasciata

HARDINESS ZONE AND TEMPERATURE RANGE
9b–11; 50°F–80°F

IDEAL LIGHTING
Partial shade, bright
indirect light

GROWING LOCATION
Shady outdoors/indoors

SIZE
3–5" tall; 7–8" spread

Thick, triangular leaves with dotted white stripes like drips of frosting grow in tight upturned rosettes. This plant is native to South Africa's Eastern Cape.

Special Features: Will send a dainty white (sometimes pinkish) flower with thin brown stripes far away from itself like a kite on a string. The stem can be up to 16 inches long! When stressed, the leaves will turn very red, giving it an exotic look. It will turn green again with less extreme heat.

Care Instructions: Water infrequently as the plants develop new roots of their own. You can fertilize monthly during the April to September growing season if your plant is languishing or you haven't repotted and the soil is very dry and crumbly. Don't fertilize during the dormant winter. Only water when dry; they are prone to root rot. Propagate your Zebra Plant by removing pups.

Watch Out For: Your plant will close up like a spider to conserve its energy if it is thirsty. Black spots forming on the leaves are a sign of overwatering. Common bugs to keep an eye out for are mealybugs and spider mites.

Arrangement Tips: Will look great in a small planter that matches the petite stature of the plant. Looks great in just about anything, but pay attention to the coloring of the dish. It will look modern and sculptural in a black pot, wild and natural in terra-cotta, and clean and organized in white.

COOPER'S HAWORTHIA

AKA PUSSY FOOT, WINDOW HAWORTHIA

Haworthia cooperi var. obtusa

HARDINESS ZONE AND TEMPERATURE RANGE
9b–12; 50°F–90°F

IDEAL LIGHTING
Partial shade, bright indirect light

GROWING LOCATION
Shady outdoors in warm climates/indoors

SIZE
1–3" tall; 4–6" spread with pups

Another haworthia native to South Africa's Eastern Cape. Many varietals of cooperi have a buried stem and gelatinous, translucent, and veiny leaves that just reach the surface of the soil. These leaves are sometimes referred to as "windows" because you can see through them deep into the plant. The windows allow light to reach the photosynthetic cells, which, unlike in most plants, are buried deep within the leaf.

Special Features: Will flower similarly to *Haworthia fasciata*. In different varietals, the leaves will display many colors in the windows, from oranges to reds, yellows, and purples.

Care Instructions: Propagate your haworthia by removing pups. Water infrequently while it develops new roots. It needs a minimal amount of fertilizer in the spring and fall to strengthen it for the growing season and prop it up during the dormant winter. Only water when dry; the plant is prone to root rot.

Watch Out For: It's a slow grower, so don't expect this plant to look very different over the first year or two.

Arrangement Tips: Pot it depending on the different coloring of your plant. Make sure to place it near a window where you will be able to watch the sun shine through it.

HORSE'S TEETH

Haworthia truncata

HARDINESS ZONE AND TEMPERATURE RANGE
10-15; 55°F-75°F

IDEAL LIGHTING
Full sun, partial shade

GROWING LOCATION
Indoors

SIZE
1" tall; 4" clumping spread

Native to the Little Karoo region of the Western Cape of South Africa, this plant blooms between spring and summer, sending out small, long-stemmed flowers similar to its other family members. In nature, these flowers are fertilized by bees, which could explain why this plant doesn't tend to bloom much inside.

Special Features: One of the strangest-looking succulents, the Truncata features rectangular leaves arranged similarly to the *Aloe plicatilis*, in two opposite rows. The plant gets its name from the word "truncate," as the grayish-green leaves look like they've been topped off, like a flattop hairdo.

Care Instructions: This plant is most active during spring and in late summer leading into the fall. Water less during the high summer and in the winter. Its seeds are easy to germinate, and it is also easy to propagate by dividing the pups. You can propagate this plant with its leaves, but it will take months before roots emerge. Keep it dry in the meantime.

Watch Out For: Root rot, mealybugs. Don't overwater, and treat it right away if you see the fuzzy white clumps that distinguish those bugs.

Arrangement Tips: This plant looks so interesting, it doesn't need a special pot. Perhaps terra-cotta would best highlight this unusually shaped plant. Put it in a place where you will look at it, and it may provoke philosophical thoughts.

LITTLE WARTY

AKA COW TONGUE

Gasteria batesiana x Gasteria 'Old Man Silver'

HARDINESS ZONE AND TEMPERATURE RANGE
9a-11: down to 25°F

IDEAL LIGHTING
Full sun to partial shade

GROWING LOCATION
Outdoors/indoors

SIZE
6-8" tall: 6-8" wide

A gasteria native to South Africa, this is similar to a haworthia and will grow in the same conditions. It is a great indoor succulent as long as it receives bright light and moderate water during its active months in the spring and summer.

Special Features: Larger than the dwarf bicolor, Little Warty has very thick, almost plastic-feeling stemless leaves featuring swirls of dark and light green with creamy mottling in the center.

Care Instructions: Drought-tolerant, it likes to be left fairly dry during the winter months and a bit moist during the summer and spring. It is known to flourish with monthly liquid fertilizer feeders during those growth months. In spring, when it fills its pot, repot in a slightly larger but still shallow vessel.

Watch Out For: Gasterias are susceptible to fungus and mealybugs, so water sparingly, keeping the moisture in the soil and not on the plant. Track and treat any bugs on the plant.

Arrangement Tips: Contrast with Dasyphyllum or Cape Blanco Sedum. Outside, plant under taller succulents like aeoniums or aloes. Plant alone in small planters that will match the scale of the plant, and make sure your planter has drainage.

OX TONGUE

AKA DWARF TONGUE

Gasteria bicolor var. liliputana

HARDINESS ZONE AND TEMPERATURE RANGE
9a–11; down to 25°F

IDEAL LIGHTING
Partial shade to full sun

GROWING LOCATION
Outdoors/indoors

SIZE
3–5" tall; 4–6" spread

Native to the Eastern Cape of South Africa, this gasteria grows well indoors with bright light and moderate water in the spring and summer.

Special Features: Its reptilian thick, fleshy leaves, dark green and mottled with creamy markings, are shaped like tongues. Liliputana is the dwarf version of this plant; other versions can get quite a bit larger. It makes pretty flowers in midwinter to spring that are reddish pink and full of nectar. The plant is long-stemmed and can send the blooms up to 5 feet away from their tiny parent.

Care Instructions: Drought-tolerant, it likes to be left fairly dry during the winter months and a bit moist during the spring and summer. It is known to flourish with monthly liquid fertilizer feeders during those growth months. In spring, when it fills its pot, repot in a slightly larger but still shallow vessel.

Watch Out For: Can get fungal infections from too much water, or even from water on its leaves. This will manifest with black spots on the leaves. The plant can fight back and recover from this if the conditions that caused it are altered. Generally, this means less humidity and more careful waterings. It can also be susceptible to mealybugs, so treat accordingly.

Arrangement Tips: Grow indoors in shallow planters and outdoors under taller plants that will provide shade. Will turn reddish when stressed, so give it a small amount of direct sun if you can.

ESSENTIAL SUCCULENTS

ALOE VERA
Aloe barbadensis

HARDINESS ZONE AND TEMPERATURE RANGE
10-11; down to 35°F-40°F

IDEAL LIGHTING
Full sun, partial sun, partial shade

GROWING LOCATION
Outdoors/indoors

SIZE
1-2' tall; 2-3' wide

Humans have been using Aloe Vera for skin-care and in cosmetics for at least 2,000 years. It is native to the Arabian Peninsula but grows in the wild all over the planet. It is an easy plant to grow inside or outside. It makes long, tubular yellow-green flowers, but usually only when grown outdoors.

Special Features: The sap of the thick leaves of this aloe is a great treatment for burns and light abrasions, making it a popular houseplant among parents.

Care Instructions: Outdoors this is a drought-tolerant plant that needs little care. Give it some irrigation during the hottest months and less during the winter. Indoors, water moderately, also tapering off during winter. Propagates most easily through division of offsets, which will pop up either right next to the plant or a few inches away. To keep a container plant happy, be sure to remove and replant offsets every three or four years.

Watch Out For: Scale and mealybugs are possibilities. Though Aloe Vera has a beautiful flower, it rarely blooms as an indoor plant. Brown tips on your leaves can be a sign of not enough water, and black tips can mean too much water. If you live somewhere that's cold in the winter, bring this plant outside in the spring, but be careful to acclimate it slowly to the sun, as it is surprisingly prone to sunburn. Sunburned leaves won't kill the plant, but the damage won't go away until it makes new leaves.

Arrangement Tips: Outside, this is a great border plant, and it will look especially nice in rock gardens and around boulders. Inside, it will provide height in small container gardens and will also look lovely alone in a terra-cotta pot on the kitchen windowsill.

ALOE BLUE ELF

AKA ALOE CALIFORNIA

Aloe 'Blue Elf'

HARDINESS ZONE AND TEMPERATURE RANGE
9–11; 20°F–100°F

IDEAL LIGHTING
Full sun, partial shade

GROWING LOCATION
Outdoors/indoors

SIZE
12–18" tall; 2' spread

A clumping aloe that can live in extreme heat, it has straight-standing grayish-blue leaves and creates a spike of orange flowers throughout winter that can be tinged with red in very hot climates. Known to flower intermittently all year long.

Special Features: This aloe has elegant foliage; its ability to withstand heat and drought make it a fabulous landscaping plant. It is not known exactly where it comes from. Aloes are native to the African continent, and some experts think the Blue Elf originated in South Africa, but others say it was farther north, possibily on the Canary or Cape Verde Islands.

Care Instructions: Outdoors it needs only intermittent water during the hottest months. Indoors, water every two weeks or when the soil is dry. When the Blue Elf is not getting as much sun as it loves, its foliage will turn greener, and it may not flower.

Watch Out For: Not prone to many pests or diseases. Don't plant under trees, which can drop pest-ridden foliage onto the leaves. If the leaves are yellowing or drying at the tips, use a high-phosphate fertilizer in the early winter to promote those gorgeous blooms. Don't forget to prune the stalks when they are done flowering.

Arrangement Tips: If you have lots of space, this can be a great ground cover, as it's known to create a ton of offsets and clump beautifully. It looks stunning when an entire patch is in bloom; attracts hummingbirds and other garden life.

THE 50 BEST SUCCULENT VARIETIES FOR BEGINNERS

FAN ALOE

Aloe plicatilis or Kumara plicatilis

HARDINESS ZONE AND TEMPERATURE RANGE
9–11; down to 20°F–25°F

IDEAL LIGHTING
Full sun, partial sun

GROWING LOCATION
Outdoors/indoors

SIZE
Typically grows to 4-8' tall and spreads 4-6' wide, but known to grow up to 16' tall in the wild.

Plicatilis is a Latin term meaning "foldable" or "pleated." The leaves of this plant don't fold, but they look like an extended fan. The plant will typically grow like a tree, or a caudiciform-like shrub (see Glossary), with a bulbous base above the soil and a barky gray trunk rising from the ground. Native to South Africa, this fascinating aloe sends out sets of blue-gray leaves curving into one another in a fanlike pattern.

Special Features: The leaves are attractive, and with full sun can be translucent at the tips, glowing a reddish orange. The Fan Aloe's tubular red flowers will typically bloom between spring and fall in the United States, but can also appear in the other seasons. The bark is quite fire-resistant, so it is a good plant for dry regions prone to wildfires.

Care Instructions: Outdoors it will want water in the winter and early spring, so irrigate if you live in a drier climate. Indoors it will need as much brightness as possible. The leaves will naturally turn black and fall off, revealing the smooth young bark below. However, inside, if your leaves are turning mushy before turning black, this could mean your plant is not getting enough light or is getting too much water with not enough drainage. It is a slow grower either outdoors or indoors, and is easily propagated through stem or branch cuttings (remember to let them dry before replanting).

Watch Out For: Root rot from wet soil; mealybugs and scale, which can be treated with a neem oil–based spray.

Arrangement Tips: The Fan Aloe's fancy shape makes it a remarkable plant, so it will look elegant wherever you place it. It is great in large decorative containers, with agaves and senecios as companions. It looks fantastic as part of any outdoor landscaping, especially when its tubular blooms are in full swing.

RED YUCCA

Hesperaloe parviflora

HARDINESS ZONE AND TEMPERATURE RANGE
5-11; down to -20°F-45°F

IDEAL LIGHTING
Full sun

GROWING LOCATION
Outdoors

SIZE
3-5' tall; 3' wide

This is not actually a yucca, but a member of the agave family. It has green foliage in the summer, which can turn plum-colored in the winter. The leaves have an interesting frayed, fibrous fringe along their spines. This plant is a slow grower and is respected for its incredible ability to withstand cold winters. It is found in nature from southern Texas to northern Mexico.

Special Features: Its blooms of tubular reddish flowers crowding showy pink stalks have been known to last more than four weeks and will attract hummingbirds and bees. In warm-winter regions, these blooms can come year-round; otherwise expect them in early summer.

Care Instructions: This plant only needs moderate watering. It will want a regular drink in extreme heat or when in containers, but mostly likes to be left alone in regions where it will get winter rain. Remove the flower stalks when the bloom is dried. Propagates best from seed.

Watch Out For: The succulent leaves are tasty to grazing deer, so protect them when young, and enjoy the fauna when the plants are full size and out of danger.

Arrangement Tips: In desert landscapes, these are terrific xeriscape plants. They look great in rock gardens and grassland gardens. Plant near boulders and use small plants like sedums and sempervivums as companions, along with bolder plants with similarly striking flowers, like Bird of Paradise. The Red Yucca will also thrive in containers in smaller gardens, in the front of your house as a greeter, or in the back on a stone patio.

PARRY'S AGAVE

AKA ARTICHOKE AGAVE

Agave parryii var. huachucensis

HARDINESS ZONE AND TEMPERATURE RANGE
5–11; known to survive cold
temperatures down to -20°F

IDEAL LIGHTING
Full sun, filtered sun

GROWING LOCATION
Outdoors

SIZE
2' by 2', with a flowering
stalk that can reach 15' tall

An agave native to Mexico and the southwest United States, this plant will take 10 to 20 years to attain full growth, at which point it flowers magnificently and then dies.

Special Features: Has very pretty grayish-blue leaves with sharp teeth along the spine of each leaf and a sharp spine on the end. The top of the leaf will have a brownish color. When the plant flowers, it will send a large treelike stalk from the center of the plant that eventually forms 20 to 30 branches, each with a large cluster of yellow flowers. The fermented pulp of this plant can be distilled to make mezcal and tequila.

Care Instructions: Requires very little care outdoors; once established, it will not need to be watered. Cannot be propagated with leaves, but you can collect offsets somewhat regularly.

Watch Out For: Prone at times to scale, a bug that attaches itself to the underside of plant leaves; this can be treated with an insecticidal soap or a neem oil spray. Also must have a gritty, sandy planting mix or can form root rot.

Arrangement Tips: Because it is such a hardy plant, it makes a great landscape pick in wintry areas. Plant in groupings with about 3 feet of space between them.

VARIEGATED FOX TAIL AGAVE

Agave attenuata 'Kara's Stripes'

HARDINESS ZONE AND TEMPERATURE RANGE
10-12; down to 35°F

IDEAL LIGHTING
Full sun, partial sun, full shade

GROWING LOCATION
Outdoors

SIZE
2-4' tall; 3-6' spread

This agave's translucent yellowish-green leaves form soft rosettes that tilt slightly upward toward the sky, as if looking into the sun. *Agave attenuata* is native to Mexico.

Special Features: Thought to be a slow grower, Kara's Stripes will live for around 20 years, at which point the monocarpic plant will send up its 10- to 15-foot flower stalk and finish its life in a show of fragrant yellow-green flowers. The stalk, unlike the straight asparagus shape of many other agave plants, frequently bends over and dips down, forming an arch.

Care Instructions: There is little to do for this easy agave. It is frost-sensitive, so cover with frost cloth during a cold spell. It is heat-tolerant, but would love some afternoon shade if the temperature is very warm, so plant accordingly.

Watch Out For: Overwatering is a concern. In general, it won't need any water during the dormant winter months.

Arrangement Tips: Its bright, colorful appearance, which will improve in good sun, makes it a crowd-pleaser in any garden setting. It would be majestic planted alone in a wine barrel planter. Alongside sedums and aeoniums, it will be a point of focus. Kara's Stripes will help delineate spaces when planted along fences with aloes and other agaves.

QUEEN VICTORIA AGAVE
Agave victoriae-reginae

HARDINESS ZONE AND TEMPERATURE RANGE
9–11; 15°F–90°F

IDEAL LIGHTING
Full sun

GROWING LOCATION
Outdoors/indoors; must have great sun indoors

SIZE
18" x 18"

Compact dark-green rosettes with intricate white markings make this a very showy plant. It's ideal as a specimen or isolated with boulders and only smaller plants around it. Most varieties do not have marginal teeth on the leaves, but do have a 1- to 3-inch thorn at the end of each leaf. Native to Mexico.

Special Features: Like most agaves, it will bloom once after 10 to 25 years with a thick stalk covered in dense greenish-white flowers tinged with purples and reds.

Care Instructions: Loves a gritty, well-draining soil. Water it about once a month inside, when dry. Outside, water rarely, only once a month during hot seasons and not at all during the winter. Loves the heat but is also very hardy in the cold. Propagate by removing offsets. Will also give you seedpods when the flower is done; allow the pods to dry before opening and removing the seeds.

Watch Out For: Use caution when dealing with agaves. Although this one does not have marginal teeth, the spikes on the ends of each leaf will leave a painful reminder if you get poked. Use gloves, and wear long pants and solid shoes when transplanting. Mostly pest-free, but as with most agaves, look for scale and treat immediately.

Arrangement Tips: Put it in a planter at your front door, or in a living room high off the ground where no one can poke themselves on it. Set around boulders in a yard, but not with other large shrubs that can obscure it from view. Plant low succulents of solid blues and oranges around it to show off its pretty markings.

GHOST EUPHORBIA

AKA AFRICAN CANDELABRA, THE PALE EUPHORBIA

Euphorbia ammak 'Variegata'

HARDINESS ZONE AND TEMPERATURE RANGE
9a-11: down to 35°F

IDEAL LIGHTING
Full sun to partial shade

GROWING LOCATION
Outdoors/indoors

SIZE
15-30' tall; 6-12' wide

African Candelabra is actually not found on continental Africa but on the Arabian Peninsula, specifically Saudi Arabia and Yemen. The variegated version of the euphorbia grows tall and spreads its branches to resemble a giant candelabra.

Special Features: It features marbling variegated patterns in its yellow-whitish flesh, with reddish-brown edging and spines. The yellow-green flowers that emerge on top in spring will give way to an inedible greenish fruit.

Care Instructions: This slow grower wants some shade in very hot climates and will grow a little faster with regular summer water. It wants to get dry in between waterings to avoid root rot. This succulent does not love the wind, so plant in a protected location. You can prune it for shape and form. Don't forget to propagate the cuttings, which should re-root in soil after being allowed to dry and scab over.

Watch Out For: Most euphorbias feature an irritating milky sap that can damage your eyes, so use gloves and eye gear when handling and pruning this plant. Ghost Euphorbia has been known to topple over with too much water, wind, or a combination of both.

Arrangement Tips: Grow in a container inside in a bright, sunny corner. Outdoors, grow as a focal point in a sunny spot protected from the wind.

NOPALES

AKA NOPALITO, PRICKLY PEAR

Opuntia ficus-indica 'Burbank Spineless'

HARDINESS ZONE AND TEMPERATURE RANGE
9–11; 15°F–100°F

IDEAL LIGHTING
Full sun

GROWING LOCATION
Outdoors/indoors

SIZE
10–15' tall; 5–10' wide

This Mexican native features oblong blue-green leaves commonly referred to as pads (actually called "thalli"). The leaves are mostly spineless and will create showy yellow-gold flowers that produce an edible fruit similar in taste to a watermelon.

Special Features: This plant is very versatile. The pads are edible raw or cooked. They can be dried to create a flour used to make cakes, squeezed to extract an anti-inflammatory gel, juiced for raw or fermented beverages, or preserved into jams and candies.

Care Instructions: An established plant needs little support. Give it some summer water in high heat (over 80°F); otherwise leave it alone. In spring, plant pads (you can even use those purchased from a grocery store) directly in the soil about a third of the way up the leaf, so that your plant has time to establish before the cold months come around. It will grow in resiliency over time.

Watch Out For: This cactus is not prone to pests or disease. Make sure to remove the hairy patches of small spines called glochids if you are harvesting the pads for consumption. You can burn them off if you are grilling; otherwise peel or scrub them with an abrasive brush under cold water.

Arrangement Tips: This is an amazing specimen plant and is great for privacy walls. It is also fire-resistant because it is so full of water. The plant is drought-tolerant and good to use for xeriscaping. Place it next to a large boulder for a dramatic effect.

Chapter Two

INDOOR & CONTAINER GARDENS

In this chapter, we will learn how to grow succulents indoors and in containers, and we will see firsthand how these plants enrich our homes and our lives with their beauty. Growing succulents indoors can present a few challenges, but with the right light, soil, and irrigation your plants will absolutely thrive.

PLACING YOUR PLANTS

Succulents have evolved in extreme climates where there is a lack of regular rainfall. They've evolved to fend for themselves, and that is how we want to nurture them. When placing new plants and planters, choose a bright, luminous spot. Plants listed as needing full sun or partial sun will want as much direct light as they can get inside. If you are planting an echeveria to enjoy in your home, it should get at least four hours of constant sun. Morning sun is less hot and harsh then afternoon sun, and this will suit your plants. Terrariums will collect and magnify heat, so place them somewhere bright, but not in direct sun. These pointers will help your plants stay happy and healthy and not get leggy or drop leaves. Our favorite families of indoor succulents are haworthia, gasteria, and aloe, all of which are partial-sun succulents with thick skin that can withstand partial shade. Although they also love full sun, cacti will do well inside, as long as they aren't overwatered. Planters with drainage holes are recommended so that your plants don't sit in wet soil. This can bring on root rot and other plant problems.

CHOOSING SOIL

A funny thing about succulents is that they have a bit of a drinking problem. They don't know when enough is enough, and they can drink so much water that they form a rot under the soil that comes up into the plant. If you catch this early, you can use your propagation skills (see chapter 4) to save the plant, but the rot itself will not go away. As a result, succulents do best in a chunky, well-draining soil that doesn't hold water. Succulent soil (aka cactus soil) is widely available at nurseries and hardware stores. It is also simple to make at home by mixing potting soil with **pumice** (see Glossary) or vermiculite, or even very small pebbles. The idea is to create space in the soil for the water to run through, preventing your plant from harming itself with too much drinking.

You can add some creativity by top-dressing your planting with mulch, moss, or pebbles. This will have the dual benefit of looking attractive and holding some moisture in. This won't work for plants far away from a light source, but it is a fine idea for window plantings that receive many hours of direct sun, as it mimics the plants' natural environment.

POTTING AND REPOTTING

Changing the container for your plant is a part of plant parenthood. Not only is it sometimes necessary, it is also rewarding. You may have a new plant in a plastic pot or a well-loved one that has outgrown its planter, or maybe you have a bug infestation that requires completely new soil. When choosing your planter, weigh a few factors:

▶ Make sure the one you pick has a drainage hole and a dish for underneath the plant, so that water doesn't leak all over your table or floor.

▶ Choose a container whose color, shape, and design will complement the plant it will hold.

▶ Succulents like to grow to the size of their planter, so pick something that reflects your desired size for the plant.

Now that you are ready to pot, follow these steps:

1. Gather your materials somewhere easy to clean—a back deck or kitchen counter will do—or cover a table with some paper or an old tablecloth.

2. Give your new pot a good wipe to make sure it is fresh and ready.

3. Cover the bottom with drainage rock and, if you have it, add a few teaspoons of **horticultural charcoal** (see Glossary), a great maintenance tool for any succulent planting. Add a few inches of succulent soil to the bottom of your planter.

4. Now move your attention to the current planter. If you have any topdressing, carefully shift that off into a separate bowl or dish.

5. Use a flat trowel, or even a butter knife, to go around the edge of the planter to loosen the plant. Tip the pot at a slight angle and, holding the base of the plant, slide it out of the planter. It is possible the entire plant and full root ball will come up. If that is the case, slide it right over into the new vessel. If not, add more soil to the new planter so that your plant will sit at the right height in its new home.

6. At this point, check to see if you put enough soil, or too much, down at the bottom of your new planter. If it's too much, lift the plant and remove some soil so that it sits in the planter a little below the rim. If there isn't enough, add more soil below the plant and around the sides to bring the plant up to the right height. Press down with your fingers until the soil is compacted and completely filled in. Now your plant is ready for new growth and expansion.

Note: If you are working with a cactus, don't just grab it with your hands; most will leave you with a painful memento. Use leather garden gloves if you have them, or cut up a paper bag and wrap it around the cactus before you gently lift it.

WATERING AND FERTILIZING

All living things need water, and succulents are no different. But we must keep in mind their propensity to drink too much, and only give them what they need. You should consult the guidelines in chapter 1 about specific plants. For the most part, the smallest plants need to be watered every seven to 10 days, decreasing the frequency as they get larger. Even more importantly, they want to be dry before you water again. Touch the soil: Is it moist at all? Leave it alone. Is it dry at least 2 inches down? Time to water. When your succulent is thirsty, you will see its leaves start to pucker, like fingers and toes after a bath. Unfortunately, the main sign of overwatering is rot, and often when you first notice, it is too late. With both over- and under-watering, you may see yellowed leaves. This can also mean that your plant has used all the nutrients in its soil and needs to be repotted. Get on a regular watering schedule that follows the seasons, and stick to it. Water every two weeks in the spring and summer, but only when the soil is dry. During the winter months, drop down to every three to four weeks, depending on the plant. When watering a plant with a dish below it, make sure you empty the dish after it drains to prevent it from absorbing too much water.

Fertilizer can be used to keep the soil fresh and the plant happy. We generally

Troubleshooting Common Issues

PROBLEM	CAUSE	SOLUTION
Plant is getting leggy.	Too far away from the light source.	Put it in better light as soon as possible.
Dry and shriveling.	Too much light.	Move it farther away from the light.
Drying quickly after watering.	Needs to be repotted.	Get a larger pot and transplant.
Brown, green, or beige bumps on stems, often accompanied by a sticky nectar.	Scale insects.	Isolate the plant from other plants, outside if possible. Spray it down with isopropyl alcohol and scrape off the scales gently with your thumb. Repot with fresh soil.
White clumps at the base of the leaves.	Mealybugs.	Use cotton swabs and either isopropyl alcohol or a neem oil spray to clean them off. Repot with fresh soil.
Holes in leaves.	Snails or slugs.	Find and remove the pests. If the problem persists, wrap the planter with copper slug tape (available at most garden stores). The pests won't cross the copper and can't get to the leaves they want to eat.
Wet spots on the stems.	Overwatering.	Take cuttings from the plant above the mushiness and propagate those pieces. Throw away the infected plant, including the soil.
Colorful leaves turning green.	Not enough sun, too much attention (meaning water, nutrient-rich soil, and fertilizer).	Give it less attention to bring back those pretty colors.
Drying bottom leaves.	Not a problem. This is how the plant interacts with the earth to both protect itself and create detritus, which will decompose and add to the soil.	You can leave alone, or remove the leaves if you wish.
Brown marks on the tops of the leaves.	Sunburn.	Succulents can get sunburned at times. Move your plant away from the direct sun. The burns won't heal, but your plant will eventually replace those leaves.

recommend fertilizing twice a year: during early spring to encourage those flowers, and during fall in anticipation of the harsh winter. I like to use an organic liquid fertilizer, high in calcium, which succulents love. Be sure to follow the manufacturer's instructions carefully. Too much fuel is not good for plants, so just give them what the maker suggests.

MAINTAINING YOUR PLANTS

Whether through a regular watering schedule, sun nourishment, fertilization, or just a little trim every now and then, we must care for the living things around us lest they become fallow. Succulents will drop leaves for a variety of reasons. Once you see a leaf drying up, it is fine to pinch it off with your fingers or snip it with sharp scissors. If your plant is getting huge, you might decide to repot it, propagate it, or just manicure it. When I am having a problem with my plants, I frequently move them around my house to find the right spot for them. Maybe they are getting a little too much sun, or not enough. If you live in a cold or wet climate, bring your less hardy succulents (such as echeveria, crassula, and aloe) inside for the winter.

If you notice a soft, wet spot on the stem of your plant, this is a sign of rot and you must deal with it quickly. Cut the plant about a half inch above the wet spot. The wet spot and the rest of the plant below it, including the soil, can be removed from the pot and discarded. Follow the propagation instructions in chapter 4 to root and regrow your plant from the cutting you have taken.

Seasonal Care

Many succulents have growth cycles in the spring and summer. These are good months to fertilize, which will encourage that growth and maybe even the production of flowers. This is also an ideal time for propagation, as the plant is already programmed to grow and fortify itself. If you need to repot, do that in late winter so as not to interrupt this cycle. Most succulents will also require less water during those quiet winter months. There are some exceptions to this rule, such as aeoniums, which are winter growers and may look dormant during the summer.

Chapter Three

OUTDOOR GARDENS

Now it's time to get our hands into the outdoor soil. Succulents let you create a beautiful landscape in your own backyard that requires minimal maintenance and saves money on water. Best of all, many succulents will need little attention once they are established. Ready to grab those gardening gloves and head outside?

PLACING YOUR PLANTS

As you take a look at your yard and ask yourself where your plants should go, there are a number of considerations to keep in mind:

▶ Where does the sun cross the yard? Make sure to locate the direct sun, partial sun, and shade areas for your planting plan.

▶ Are there already planting beds established in the yard? If so, make sure to augment the soil for succulents if necessary.

▶ Where can a plant be placed to grow large over time and not be in the way? This is where to plant agaves, large aloes, and cacti.

▶ What are your plans for long-term growth? Leave room for that expansion around your plants.

▶ How hot and cold will it get year-round in your yard? Make sure to use plants as cold hardy as necessary for your zone, and also choose ones that can take as much sun and heat as they might get in that location.

▶ Since succulents are sun-worshipping plants, light is a crucial consideration. Remember, all "full-sun" areas are not created equal. Full sun in a place where the temperature can reach 95°F will be quite different from full sun where it never surpasses 75°F. Take this into consideration to avoid sun-burned leaves when placing echeveria, graptoveria, aeonium, and other "moderate" full-sun plants. (They like direct sunlight, but not when the heat is extreme, say, 90°F or above.)

▶ Look at the plant profile to see if your flora likes a little shade, too.

▶ Augment with pumice if the soil is dense but not rocky. Succulents want water, but they also want it to drain away after they get a good drink.

CHOOSING SOIL

Succulents require excellent drainage to survive. They don't like soil that will hold water; instead, they want the water to come through, allowing their roots to drink what is necessary and then move on. To test your soil for drainage, dig a hole and fill it with water. If the water doesn't drain within 30 to 45 minutes, you will need to augment the soil. Succulents don't want to be coddled, so even if you have a well-nurtured planting bed in place, you still may need to add succulent soil, or even just pumice, vermiculite, or sand, to what you already have. Certain challenging soils, like clay, may require a deeper hole to be filled with a couple inches of pumice below your plants. Rough, rocky soil should be fine.

Topdressing is a good way to create eye-catching succulent displays. Mulch can be very helpful by providing a neat, organized look; it also supports plants in very hot locations by preventing water evaporation and eventually breaking down to augment the soil with nutrients. Use large rocks as a topdressing to hide rocky,

Plant Hardiness Zones

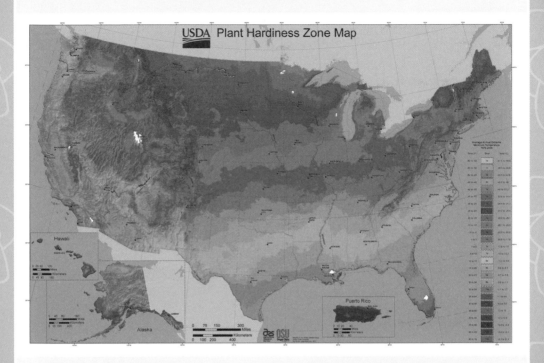

USDA Plant Hardiness Zone Map

Hardiness zones are the accepted standards to help determine which plants will thrive in your area. The map is based on minimum winter temperatures and divided into zones that are about 10 degrees apart. Most succulents love zones 9-11, where there is moderate weather and rainfall isn't too heavy. But there are exceptions to any rule. For those of you in zones 5-8, here are some great cold-tolerant succulents:

- *Agave parryi*
- *Agave victoria-reginae*
- *Sempervivum arachnoideum*
- *Sempervivum tectorum*
- *Crassula arborescens*
- *Sedum dasyphyllum*
- *Sedum rubrotinctum*
- *Sedum spathulifolium "Cape Blanco"*
- *Delosperma cooperi*
- *Hesperaloe parviflora*
- *Opuntia ficus-indica*

To view this map online and find your local hardiness zone, visit https://planthardiness.ars.usda.gov.

clunky soil. Smaller pebbles will complement more colorful succulents as they rise like a tableau from the garden floor. Try using different-colored pebbles in different locations for a stylized look.

PLANTING

Now that you're ready to create a succulent garden, gather your materials. You'll need:

▶ A good shovel

▶ A trowel

▶ Gardening gloves

▶ Some buckets to house the soil you dig out

▶ Compost bags for any other detritus

▶ Gardening scissors for manicuring

▶ Your new plants

▶ Mulch or other topdressing

▶ Optional: a larger rock or two to create ambiance around your plants

▶ Other optional materials: a water bottle, good music or a podcast to listen to, and hopefully a friend to share the work

Before you begin, have a good design prepared (for guidance, see chapter 5) along with an implementation plan. Know where each element will go, based on the considerations we discussed earlier in the chapter, such as where the sun is and which plants will get large and which will stay small. Set the plants down

in their spot and view the layout from different perspectives to see how it looks. Be flexible; sometimes a plan needs to be adjusted. Start planting toward the back of your bed and work your way forward. Enjoy the process; you are designing an area of beauty to appreciate for years to come.

When planting individual succulents, dig a hole a little bigger than the plastic planter your plant is in. Plan on sprinkling some succulent soil or pumice into the hole before you put your plant in. Remove the plant from its pot, and pull and tug a little at the roots to disrupt them a bit, which will encourage new growth once it's planted. If it is a large plant, use your scissors on both sides of the root ball and make several cuts into the roots on the outer edge. Set your plant in and fill the hole with succulent soil. If compatible, use some of the soil you dug out. Pat it down firmly, then repeat the process until all your plants are settled.

WATERING AND FERTILIZING

When you initially plant your succulents, don't water them for the first week, then give them a good soak. Regular watering may be less crucial later, depending on where you live and how much rain you get. If you live in a moderate climate with a mild but active rainy season, it may not be necessary at all. If you live in a very hot, dry climate, water your plants about twice a month during the spring and summer,

and monthly during the winter. Most succulents will be fine if watered with a hose on a shower setting. Spend five to 10 seconds on the soil around them. Because they are fragile, the littlest ones would prefer either in-ground irrigation or a gentler hose setting. In general, water in the early morning or in the late afternoon, before or after the hottest times of the day. Watering during the heat will waste water, as some will evaporate before the plants even have a chance to drink it.

Many succulents don't require any fertilization. If you want to fertilize in a moderate climate, the two seasons we recommend doing it are in the fall, to help fortify the plants for the winter, and in early spring, to incentivize those gorgeous succulent flowers we are always waiting for. In hotter climates, it is more important to fortify the plants. If you want to use a chemical fertilizer, find something organic, with a ratio of 5:5:5 or less. This refers to the percentages of nitrogen, phosphorus, and potassium in the mix. You could also use a standard seaweed fish emulsion fertilizer, which has all the nutrients succulents need. Follow the instructions carefully. Plants like food, but they don't want to be overfed. Once or twice a month during their growing cycle, usually spring and summer, should be enough. Don't feed them when they are dormant; they can't digest while they are hibernating.

MAINTAINING YOUR PLANTS

When thinking about the maintenance of your plants, decide if you prefer a natural "wild" look or a more manicured one. If you like your nature natural, maintenance will involve watching for bugs and weeds and trimming dead leaves and flowers. If you want your garden to be very organized, you will be trimming and pruning as well.

Some succulents, such as Blue Senecio, have a defined growing season, and those plants will want to be cut back each winter to promote fresh, healthy growth. Blooming succulents will require trimming the dead flower spikes after they have dried. Pull weeds that come up around your plants, taking care to get the roots if you can, so they won't come up again. Mulch will help keep weeds away over time. Watch for infestations and fungal infections, and treat them accordingly. Succulents are relatively pest-free, so those problems will be the exceptions, not the rules. Once your plants are established, you will get lots of new growth, which you can enjoy as is. Or you can propagate those plants, and soon you'll have many more plants to put around your yard, plant in containers, or give as gifts to friends and family.

Troubleshooting Common Problems

PROBLEM	CAUSE	SOLUTION
Leaves and branches are being eaten.	Some critter (for example, a deer, squirrel, or raccoon) is chomping your plant.	Cover it in chicken wire and see if that solves the problem.
Holes around the plant and leaves are wilting.	Gophers or other underground beasts.	Dig up your plants and replant using gopher-proof cages.
Leaves are wilted and yellowing.	Could be overwatering or under-watering.	Check the soil. If it is dry, water more regularly. If it is very wet, don't water again until it gets dry.
Brown, green, or beige bumps on stems.	Scale insects.	Spray it down with isopropyl alcohol, then scrape off the scales gently with your thumb. Use an organic pesticide to keep them from coming back.
White clumps at the base of the leaves.	Mealybugs.	You may need to remove and discard outdoor plants with bug infestations to prevent them from harming your other plants.
Holes in leaves.	Snails or slugs.	Find and remove the pests. If your plant is in a container, wrap the outside with copper tape (available at any garden or hardware store) to deter them.
Wet spots on the stems or leaves.	Could be frost damage.	Remove damaged plants and put frost cloth over the rest. Consider moving container succulents indoors for the winter.
Drying bottom leaves.	Not a problem. This is how the plant interacts with the earth to both protect itself and create detritus that will decompose and add to the soil.	You should leave drying leaves alone.

Chapter Four

PROPAGATING SUCCULENTS

It is quite easy to turn one succulent plant into many plants. This is called propagation, and it makes growing your collection a rewarding experience, and an inexpensive one. Propagation is what often turns succulent fans into fanatics, because one small plant can make 20 to 30 plants with just a little patience and tender loving care. Outlined in this chapter are the five ways to propagate succulents, from easiest to most challenging.

CUTTINGS

Many varieties of succulents can be propagated by snipping a little piece off the mother plant where there are new stems and growths. The piece you have removed is called a "cutting" or "stem cutting." This is the quickest and most immediately gratifying way to multiply your plants. Since succulents have difficulty monitoring their water intake, we let our new cuttings dry on a tray with bright light for at least a week. During this time, they will scab over where they were cut, and even possibly start to send out little roots. The scab will prevent the plant from taking in too much water when planted, and the roots will reach out for nutrients when it is situated in the soil. When ready, you can place the cuttings in a planter with fresh succulent soil, or directly in the ground outside. Don't water for the first two weeks; this will encourage the growth of roots to help your cutting establish itself in the soil.

Afterward, regular waterings will encourage the plant to grow and thrive. Cuttings are especially great for constructing certain types of vertical gardens planted in moss. Aeoniums, kalanchoes, crassulas, senecios, and some other succulents that grow offshoots are perfect candidates for this type of simple propagation.

LEAVES

Leaf propagation is succulent magic! Many varietals, such as echeveria, graptoveria, and graptopetalum, will reproduce entirely from one leaf. Succulents are the ultimate "will-to-live" plants; they don't want to die. They will prove that to you by reproducing leaf by leaf.

1. Separate a leaf from the mother plant as cleanly as possible (they will usually just pop off in your fingers).

2. Lay the leaf on a tray in a dry, bright environment. After a few days, you may see the first little hairy red roots sprouting from the leaf. This is an indication that your leaf is expressing its strong will to live.

3. After you get some roots, place the leaf on a bed of soil in a planter or on a tray, curved-side down and in a dry environment, and mist it with water every week. If your leaves are outside, make sure they are protected from the rain and not in direct sun.

4. Soon a miniature rosette will sprout from the base of the leaf. Now you can water it every two weeks, with just enough water to moisten the soil. Succulents

would prefer a little neglect to over nurturing.

5. Wait until a rosette is at least 1 inch wide before repotting. For most succulents, this will take about four to eight months. Plant it with succulent soil in a pot with a drainage hole.

DIVISION

Many succulent plants multiply by sending out roots along the underside of their stems, which connect with the soil and spread out along the ground. Sedums (succulent ground covers), senecios (generally known for their gorgeous dangling tendrils, such as String of Pearls and Fishhooks), and crassulae are plants that exhibit this type of growth. These plants

can grow in bushy, low clumps and are easy to separate into many plants.

First, take the plant out of its planter. Holding the plant in your hands, with your thumbs closest to you, gently use your fingers to open the plant outward, separating it first into two parts and then into however many you'd like. The plants will be in small clumps, with shallow, feathery roots slipping down into the soil.

Each of these clumps can be replanted, either separately in new pots or together in a centerpiece to highlight a larger plant. I find this to be especially fun when creating terrariums: Separate a sedum into three or four clumps and then plant them around cactus and haworthia for an elegant and manicured look.

CHICKS

Have you heard the term "hens and chicks"? It is used to describe certain types of succulent plants, generally in the echeveria and sempervivum families, that reproduce with offsets surrounding a main plant. The "hen" is the mother plant, and the "chicks" are its little offsets, sprouting up around Mom, connected with a little stem much like an umbilical cord. Aloes, haworthias, agaves, and gasterias also reproduce in this way, sending chicks (also known as pups or offsets) out into the world. Interestingly, many of these plants will not reproduce using leaf- or stem-cutting methods. However, the offsets are quite easily separated from the main plant and just need a little water and sun to grow into mature plants of their own. Repot if you wish once they are about 1 to 2 inches tall. If only human children were this easy!

SEEDS

If you have seeds, either from a package or flowers that you have dried, you have the opportunity to produce many plants at once, although this is a more challenging way to propagate succulents. Succulent seeds need soil and lots of light to germinate. They tend to be very small, so it can be easy to lose track of them when you are planting. For best results, follow these basic steps:

1. Get a seed tray (sold at garden stores) or use an empty egg carton and fill it with a nice blend of succulent soil, heavy on the pumice, to about ½ inch below the top. With clean, dry hands, place your seeds right on top of the soil. Don't worry about digging them in. Cover your seed tray with the lid; if you are using an egg carton, cover with some plastic wrap. One concern is losing the tiny seeds before they sprout. I find this to be a challenge when watering, because they can swim away with the runoff, so I like to place the tray in another larger tray filled with water and let the soil absorb the water from below.

2. Keep the soil moist as the seeds grow and develop, and make sure they have either bright indirect sun or grow lights at least 12 hours a day. Most succulent seeds will start to germinate within three weeks (though some can take much longer). Soon they will start to grow little stems and leaves. Once you can see their leaves start to plump, cut back on the water and let the soil dry between waterings.

3. Pot them up individually, or in groups of three, in fresh, well-draining succulent soil when they are about 2 to 4 inches tall, or when their rosette has developed to around that same size. Cacti can be potted when they are smaller.

Although the process is slow and can be relatively challenging, since there are so many other ways to multiply your plants, if you get good at germinating succulent seeds, you can easily have a ton of succulents for just a little money spent.

Chapter Five

DESIGN BASICS

Designing with succulents is as easy as it is fun. These colorful, architectural plants are resilient, forgiving, and require minimal maintenance. They're perfect for container gardening, outdoor landscaping, interior design, and even as wedding florals.

ESSENTIAL ELEMENTS

Consider these essential elements when designing with succulents:

Color. Succulents come in all tints and tones. Take a look at the colors of your walls, floors, and decor to devise a color palette for your plant and pot selection. You can create harmony by repeating tones, or use contrast to highlight a particular hue. Think about how the colors might change if the plants are stressed, and plan for those changes.

Size and scale. Make sure to put plants where they can grow to their optimal size without causing havoc. Sharp plants should be placed safely where they won't

poke anyone. Small plants should be positioned where they are most likely to be admired and enjoyed. Use elements that will fit their dimensions; small pebbles will look good with small rosettes, and large rocks will be in scale with larger ones. If you are pairing a snake plant with Fishhooks Senecio, make sure there is just as much room for the trailing plant to grow downward as there is for the climbing plant to grow up.

Shape. Put a cascading plant up high, where its natural growth patterns will be accented. Tall plants need to be where their growth won't be impeded, and where they can make a strong statement. Follow the patterns on the plants. Match up square leaves with square pots, and round leaves with round pots. Put round pots on round tables and rectangular pots on rectangular tables. Plant aloes to complement agaves.

Texture. Succulents have many textures, from waxy or fuzzy to barbed and pointy. Use these characteristics to make a statement. Spiky plants will project durability, so place them on heavy wooden furniture inside, or place them with just the sky as a backdrop outside.

Context. Let the objects and attributes of your space impact your design. Integrate and merge the existing trees, sculpture, art, and furniture into your ideas. Use topdressing to connect plantings with their environment or to provide a playful contrast.

OUTDOOR GARDENS

When planning your outdoor garden, decide how much space you will allot to plants. Seating areas can help delineate or punctuate your garden into zones. It might be nice to have one spot where a group of people can sit, and a smaller spot for peaceful meditation. Make sure these areas have the best views of your garden and the world beyond. Incorporate the colors and shapes of the plants, furniture, walls, and fences that are there into your design. Let some of your plant and/or planter decisions be guided by these shapes: Use square planters where lines are sharp; choose round plants and planters where you have soft curves and oval patterns. Scale is important, so make plant selections that will be appropriate once they've reached their maximum size. Don't add plants that will get very large to a small space, unless they are the focal point with a few smaller plants around them. Landscaping lights can really make your garden pop. Add them judiciously; with evening light, less is more. Use rocks, water features, sculptures, and hills to create spaces within the space. Plant in patches around a central path through the garden, using larger, bushy succulents like aloe, kalanchoe, and aeonium to make borders around patios, or along fences. Adding stone, wood, and metal elements to your design will add dimension and round out your space. For example, top-dress the entire planting area with stones of different sizes and shapes to make a basic rock garden. Add a fountain or pond to promote tranquility. Plant sedum ground covers along paths, and between stepping stones. Consider a vertical garden if your space is full and you still want some succulents outside.

Drought-Tolerant Yards

Water is a resource not readily available everywhere. Fortunately, drought-tolerant yards and xeriscapes (landscapes requiring little or zero water) can be as beautiful as they are cost-effective. Choose succulents that are especially sun and heat hardy, such as agave, cactus, sedum, and echeveria. Plant fewer but larger succulent plants in groupings throughout the yard, and choose greenery that will propagate without irrigation to fill smaller areas within your space. Manicure the topography with pebbles or crushed granite to create a desert vibe around your independent plants. Sink a few boulders into your design, perhaps one big enough to sit on to enjoy the view.

INDOOR AND CONTAINER GARDENS

There are a lot of opportunities to be creative when planting inside. Succulents will add to the ambience of any room that has sufficient light for them to thrive. Place your container gardens in rooms that will get three to four hours of bright light, preferably from the morning sun. Consider purchasing plant lights from your local garden store or online to supplement light where it is not naturally available. Color, again, will be a central theme. Connect your plants easily to their new habitat by matching their colors to the walls and furniture. Use a contrasting color with your planter to create a visual pop in a monochromatic room, or the opposite. Use colored tumbled glass to provide a playful topdressing in rooms with brightly colored walls.

If you want to get creative, I highly recommend experimenting with a variety of unusual containers. I've planted succulents in lunch boxes, ceramic mugs, teacups, teapots, popcorn poppers, glass pitchers, watering cans, shoes, and seashells, among other things. Find a whimsical vessel that fits your room's decor and turn it into a planter. If there is no drainage, and it doesn't make sense to drill or cut holes in it, use some drainage rock and horticultural charcoal to separate the plants from the water. You can also put decorative elements in the containers with your plants. Arrange chunks of colored glass, metal figures, or favorite shells on top of the soil as companions to your plants. Remember, your plants are alive, so consider their growth potential when placing them.

ESSENTIAL SUCCULENTS

Chapter Six

EASY DECORATIVE PROJECTS

Succulents are a fantastic medium for crafting. Their agreeable nature makes them easy to work with and amenable to a variety of conditions, such as being planted in moss instead of soil, growing vertically as well as horizontally, and even surviving without roots in floral arrangements. I have prepared step-by-step instructions for eight easy decorative projects that highlight the beauty and versatility of these plants. They are listed in order from easiest to more challenging, so hone your succulent skills before tackling the projects at the end. Ready to get your hands in the soil? Let's begin.

SIMPLE SUCCULENT SQUARE

Learn planting and composition basics with this easy yet rewarding project that can live outside or inside.

Materials:

5- to 6-inch square planter with a drainage hole

Succulent soil

One 2-inch *Portulacaria afra*

One 2-inch *Rhipsalis salicornioides*

One 2-inch *Sedum nussbaumerianum*

One 2-inch *Graptopetalum amethystinum*

One 2-inch *Sempervivum arachnoideum*

One 2-inch *Sedum dasyphyllum* 'Major'

½ pound of black pebbles

Optional: Horticultural charcoal, drainage rock

Step 1: Choose your pot. Pick something with a drainage hole in a warm color palette to complement the pinks, oranges, and greens of your plants. Red, purple, black, or even white are all great choices.

Step 2: If you have drainage rock and charcoal, place about ½ inch of the rock and 1 to 2 teaspoons of the charcoal down at the bottom of the planter. Fill the planter with soil to about 1 inch below the top edge.

Step 3: Take the portulacaria out of its plastic planter and give it a little squeeze to disrupt the roots. Dig a little hole against the back of the planter, in one of the corners, and place your plant in it. This plant will provide scale, mimicking a tree's role in a garden.

Step 4: Divide the rhipsalis and the *Sedum nussbaumerianum* in pieces and plant them interspersed with each other around the portulacaria. The different textures of the plants will provide contrast, and both will provide height.

Step 5: Plant the graptopetalum and the sempervivum in front, not quite in line with each other but slightly offset. Divide the *Sedum dasyphyllum* and fill in the edges of the planter with the clumps. The pinks and blues of its leaves will match the graptopetalum, and its tiny rosettes will mimic the larger ones on the other plants. →

Step 6: Using your fingers and/or the bottom of a spoon, pat all your soil down tightly. When you first water, the soil will shrink a bit if not packed. Add soil if needed to keep the entire planting just ¼ to ½ inch below the edge of the planter. Smooth out the soil.

Step 7: Use your black pebbles as a topdressing all around the edges of the planter and anywhere in the interior you can see soil.

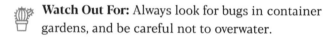

Watch Out For: Always look for bugs in container gardens, and be careful not to overwater.

Care and Maintenance: Water your garden with about ½ cup of water every 2 weeks. Give it lots of sun (at least 3 to 4 hours a day); this is especially important if you are keeping this indoors. Touch the soil before watering; if it is still moist, wait until it is dry on top before watering again.

MASON JAR TERRARIUM

A terrarium is a little world planted inside of glass. You can keep it manicured and organized, or let it grow wild and free. This easy, fun project will nurture your inner plant artist.

Materials:

A clear (not colored) mason jar, any size

1 pound drainage pebbles (multiple types are best)

1 teaspoon horticultural charcoal (not mandatory, but helpful for longevity)

Succulent soil

A few small succulents (cuttings will work; prepare them 1 week before)

A chopstick and a spoon

Some decorative elements such as reindeer moss, shells, gems, little toy animals, marbles, or sea glass

Step 1: Wash your jar in warm, soapy water and dry it thoroughly to make sure there is no residue from the previous contents. Cleaning the glass well will allow you to view your terrarium as clearly as possible.

Step 2: Put in about ½ inch to 1 inch of drainage pebbles. This can be any material that won't break down in water.

Step 3: Sprinkle your charcoal over the pebbles. This will help distribute the water more evenly.

Step 4: Put in about 1 inch of soil. It's easy to add more, but harder to take it out, so start with a small amount, just enough so that the top of your plants will be even with or below the top edge of the mason jar.

Step 5: Add your plants. If you are using cuttings, simply plant them about 1 inch into the soil, and arrange them decoratively. If using plants with root balls, gently pull them out of their plastic planters and, using your fingers, remove much of the soil around the roots. Then, using a chopstick, spoon, or your finger, make an indentation in the soil and place your plant in. Repeat for each plant.

Step 6: Pack the soil nicely around the plants by pressing down around them with a spoon or your fingers. Add a little more soil on top if necessary to cover any roots, or to bring the soil back up to the bottom of the plants. →

Step 7: Time to decorate. Your decorative elements can emphasize the secondary colors in your plants. For instance, choose something red if your Lipstick Echeveria has pronounced crimson edging. Place your materials one at a time and take a look at your creation. A little decor will go a long way, and, as with all art, knowing when you are finished is one of the fun challenges. Remember, the plants are the crowd-pleasers, so don't overshadow them with too many additions.

Watch Out For: Some of your succulents might have thick, ropy roots (haworthia, aloe, gasteria). You might have to do a little root trimming to get them into the terrarium. Don't worry; succulents are survivors. If you take a little off, they will forgive you.

Care and Maintenance: Water your terrarium with about 1 tablespoon of water every 2 weeks. The glass will magnify the heat, so place it in a bright spot that won't get direct sun.

KOKEDAMA STRING GARDEN

Plant a succulent in a mossy air garden using the ancient Japanese art of *kokedama*, "moss ball" in English. Display this in a shallow bowl, alone on a table or shelf, or hanging in the air.

Materials:

A succulent plant (or plants) of any size

Succulent soil

Moss (preferably green sheet moss, but sphagnum can work)

String or twine, any color

Scissors, for cutting the twine

Step 1: Take your plant out of its pot and set it on your workspace. Dampen some succulent soil slightly and use your hands to add it to your succulent's root balls to create a ball shape.

Step 2: With the color side of your sheet moss down, place your succulent in the center of the moss and fold the sheet up and around the entire root balls. If there are any tears in the moss, use additional pieces to seal the soil inside.

Step 3: Wrap the string around your moss ball as you would wrap yarn onto a ball, or in a design of concentric circles. Make sure you wrap it well enough to completely hold the structure together. As you wrap, use your hands to mold your kokedama into the shape you want, such as a ball or an oval.

Step 4: Tie off your string in an inconspicuous place with a double knot. If you plan on hanging the kokedama, leave an additional few feet of string coming off the knot.

Watch Out For: Think of this like a container garden, and watch out for bugs that can infest plants. As with all succulents, don't overwater. Add additional moss and retie if the sheet moss rips or disintegrates. →

Care and Maintenance: Display your kokedama in a brightly lit area where your succulent will get the light it requires, either sitting flat or hanging from a length of string. Hanging gardens will look spectacular either alone or with a few other kokedamas nearby. Create a bunch of small ones and hang them from your holiday tree as living ornaments. Water your piece weekly during the growing season by setting it in a dish of water for 4 to 5 minutes and letting it soak it up from the bottom. Water less during the dormant season. Fertilize with a liquid fertilizer at one-half or one-quarter strength, also during the growing seasons.

SUCCULENT WREATH

Create a festive, long-lasting succulent wreath using cuttings planted in moss. Make this in August or September so the cuttings are fully rooted in time to hang for the holidays.

Materials:

Mesh-covered moss wreath form (available at many garden stores and online)

Garden scissors

Succulent cuttings with 1 to 2 inches of stem at the bottom

Chopstick

Optional: garden pins (available at garden stores or online)

Step 1: The week before you compose your wreath, make your succulent cuttings by snipping off small pieces of your plants. Leave 1 to 2 inches of stem at the bottom of each cutting, if available. Trim leaves below the rosette so the stem is bare. Leave those cuttings somewhere bright but not in direct light, and wait to use them until they have calloused where they were cut.

Step 2: Soak your wreath form in a flat bowl filled with water for 20 minutes to loosen up the tightly packed moss right before you begin. This will make your moss easy to work with.

Step 3: After you decide on an arrangement, use the chopstick to poke deep holes in the moss through the mesh and slide your cuttings all the way in. Some people space them ½ inch to 1 inch apart for growth, but you can also pack them together, and they will probably all root. Start by planting your largest pieces and then fill in around them with the smaller ones.

Note: If you want, you can use floral pins to hold your plants in place, though we really recommend this project stay horizontal for at least two months, and sometimes up to four to five months, depending on how fast your plants grow roots. →

Step 4: Patience is very important when working with cuttings. There is no instant gratification, as you must wait 10 to 14 weeks for them to root and take hold in their new environment. During this time, give them plenty of bright filtered light every day. Water by soaking the entire form in a shallow bowl every 2 to 3 weeks, but each time, make sure it is completely dry beforehand.

Step 5: Once the cuttings have rooted and the wreath is filled out, hang it by a galvanized hook (to prevent rust) on your door, fence, or in a very bright window.

Watch Out For: Pro tip: Use succulents that don't get leggy, and ones that stay flat and close to the ground. This will prevent the need for regular pruning. Pay attention to the individual cuttings and make sure they aren't drying up. If you are hanging the wreath outside when complete, acclimate it slowly by gradually increasing exposure to full sun for sunburn prevention.

Care and Maintenance: A succulent wreath can last for years. Take it down and soak it in water every two to four weeks. Feed it with a liquid fertilizer in the water monthly during spring and summer. As it grows, you can manicure it for appearance. If at any point you don't like the shape, add more cuttings and begin the process again.

BIRDFEEDER VERTICAL GARDEN

This simple wire basket, widely available online and at hardware stores, is repurposed as a vertical gardening planter. I developed this beginner project as a workshop at my San Francisco store, Succulence. It is an easy introduction to planting succulents in moss, and will be ready to hang as soon as you are done.

Materials:

A suet bird feeder cage (available at hardware stores or online)

1-2 pounds of sphagnum moss

Assorted 2-inch succulents (5 to 9)

Chopsticks

5- to 7-inch bowls to use for soil (1 or 2)

Reindeer or Spanish moss for decorating

Step 1: First, shred the moss with your hands in a well-ventilated area. Open the cage and lay it flat on the other side with the chain pulled outside. Pack it solidly with your moss, fitting in as much as possible. This is the medium your plants will live in, so it needs to be sturdy. Close the cage and turn it over so the door is on the bottom.

Step 2: Plan your composition by arranging your plants in a pattern on the surface of the cage. If there are dangly plants, place them toward the bottom so they don't cover the others. I like to pick two or three varieties that repeat in horizontal, vertical, or diagonal stripes.

Step 3: Plant from one side to the other, with each plant fitting into one of the square holes (you will not plant all the holes). Pick the first spot you will place a plant and create an opening all the way to the other side of the cage by compressing the moss in all four directions with chopsticks and/or your fingers. Remove the plant from its plastic planter and remove as much soil as needed to place the entire root system into the hole so the plant is sitting snugly on the surface of the cage. →

Step 4: Fortify the plant. Using little pinches of the moss and your chopsticks, press additional sphagnum moss around the edges of and under the plant. Be careful not to break the rosette off its stem. Turn the cage upside down and gently shake it. Did your plant fall out? If so, tuck more moss around the edges of the plant. You can really get a lot of moss into the cage.

Step 5: Decorate and display. Once your plants are set, use reindeer or Spanish moss as a highlighter, either making a frame around the entire piece or pressing bits in between the plants to create a mossy background. Hang outdoors on a fence, wall, or tree. Consult your plant guide to see if you need to bring it indoors during the winter. Hang inside on a hook (so you don't damage the drywall) in a sunny spot.

Watch Out For: Make sure your succulents are nestled sturdily in the moss, tucking more moss in if necessary to hold the plants.

Care and Maintenance: Water by soaking with a hose every 10 to 14 days in the warm months and monthly during the winter. Trim dead flowers and leaves. Fertilize twice a month during the summer with a liquid fertilizer at half strength. Add to your planting if any of your plants don't survive.

SUCCULENT PUMPKIN

Mount succulents atop a pumpkin or squash to create a living seasonal centerpiece that can last for several months. Tiny pumpkins will make great host gifts. Try this project with white and/or striped pumpkins for interesting visuals.

Materials:

A pumpkin or other kind of squash, preferably with a flat top

Hot glue, craft glue, or spray adhesive, or any combination of the three

Moss, either sphagnum, Spanish, or sheet

Garden scissors

Potted small succulents or succulent cuttings

Newspaper or butcher paper to protect your table

Step 1: Coat the top of your pumpkin with a thin layer of glue. Some like to use the spray adhesive for this, but if you are using one kind of glue, choose a glue gun or craft glue that can handle all the aspects of this project. Press the moss over that glue to make a mat about ½ inch thick. If you are using a hot glue gun, make sure to press the moss down while the glue is still warm but not hot enough to burn you. You can use latex gloves for additional security.

Step 2: If using potted succulents, remove all the soil from the plants before you begin. Using garden scissors, snip away any extra stems or roots to trim the plants to the shapes and pieces you want to use. Leave a little stem on each plant, which will send out roots and help the plant propagate after the pumpkin gets soft.

Step 3: Starting with the largest succulents, glue them to the moss one at a time, working from the center outward. Glue them at the bottom, and leave some stem clear of the glue if possible, as that is where they will send out new roots. Pack them tightly for an amazing presentation. Plant the center cuttings straight up, but angle the side pieces outward for a rounded arrangement. Use some trailing succulents for a contrasting effect.

Step 4: The moss mat that you originally glued on top may or may not be aesthetically pleasing. Trim it for shape and appearance once you are finished planting. I find that leaving some mossy tendrils cascading downward looks great. →

SUCCULENT PUMPKIN, CONTINUED

Watch Out For: Keep the pumpkin dry. Don't let it sit on water or concrete, which will speed up the maturation process. Sit it on a trivet or even a piece of cardboard to give it some bottom ventilation.

Care and Maintenance: This centerpiece can last for a month or much longer. Mist it with a spray bottle every seven days, but don't saturate the plants. That will hasten rot from the squash. When the plants start to look wilted or the squash gets soft, gently peel the entire moss covering with all your succulents off. Many of the cuttings may have little roots on them already. You can plant the entire sheet of moss in a planter or outside, or plant individually.

SUCCULENT BOUTONNIERE

Use succulents to create a living boutonniere for a special occasion. Afterward, unwrap it and replant it in soil.

Materials:

A few 2-inch succulents or succulent cuttings, in colors that match your outfit

Scissors

Floral wire, gauge 18 to 30 (the lower the gauge, the thicker the wire)

Floral tape

Wire cutters

Ribbon or twine

Floral pins

Optional: Tiny flowers or foliage of any kind

Step 1: If you are using rooted plants, knock off all the soil and, using your scissors, cut off the roots and stems so that you are just working with the rosettes. If you are using cuttings, it is fine to leave the stems.

Step 2: Create a stem for your succulents with the floral wire. Push wire horizontally through the succulent's stem just below the rosette, then fold it down the other side. Or, if your plant has a small stem, wrap the wire around the base of the stem tightly, leaving a length of the wire hanging down. Repeat with a new wire for each succulent. Use the floral tape to tightly wrap each succulent to the wire.

Step 3: Choose one succulent as a focal point and arrange the other pieces around it. Use your wire cutters to trim the wires evenly to about 2 to 3 inches long. Wrap the wire stems and any other optional flowers or foliage together with floral tape.

Step 4: Wrap the taped wire with ribbon or twine and secure near the top with a floral pin. Use floral pins in the middle to attach the boutonniere to a dress or suit.

Watch Out For: Be gentle with your cuttings. Don't thread the wire too deep into the rosette, as it may break. If it does, remove the wire and use a different cutting. Root and plant the damaged cutting if possible.

Care and Maintenance: Your boutonniere will last at least a week and maybe as long as a month before it starts to wilt. You can mist it every few days to prolong its life. Afterward, unwrap the pieces and replant the cuttings in a planter. You may have plants to nurture for years to come to commemorate your special day.

SUCCULENT BICYCLE WHEEL

Create an outdoor vertical succulent garden using a discarded bicycle wheel and assorted succulents planted in sphagnum moss.

Materials:

A bicycle wheel, tube and tire removed

3 to 4 pounds sphagnum moss

Monofilament (fishing line)

Assorted succulents (10 to 30)

Chopsticks, if you'd like to have a tool

Step 1: Prepare your wheel by washing it with warm, soapy water and drying it thoroughly. Take a look at both sides of the wheel and decide which side you wish to display.

Step 2: Press the sphagnum moss tightly against the center of the wheel between the spokes. Add continuously, compressing it until there is about a 12- to 18-inch diameter of moss in the middle of the wheel, which will be around 3 to 4 inches thick.

Step 3: Secure the moss by tying one end of monofilament to one of the spokes. Bring the monofilament across the moss and loop it around the opposite spoke. Keep looping from spoke to spoke until the surface of the moss is covered in monofilament. Tie off the monofilament. If you have compressed your moss into a smaller circle than you want to plant in, add more moss and secure it with more line.

Step 4: Compose your planting. Arrange your succulents on top of the wheel until you have a design. I like to make striped, diagonal, or spiral designs with repetitions of four or five types of plants. Think about the growth habits of the plants you have chosen. Design with the future growth of the plants in mind, and space them accordingly.

Step 5: With your wheel flat on your work surface, take your plants out of their plastic pots one at a time and jostle the roots. Using chopsticks and/or your fingers, open the moss where you want to plant. You can knock some of the soil off the bottom of the plant so it will fit and be completely nestled within the moss. Plant the entire wheel, using additional moss around each succulent. →

Step 6: Create an additional webbing of monofilament under the leaves of the plants by repeating step 3 until all the plants are secured. Lift the wheel up slowly to see if all your plants are held in place. If any seem loose, use more monofilament and moss to secure them. Hang outdoors on a fence, wall, or tree. Consult your plant guide to see if you need to bring it indoors during the winter.

Watch Out For: Make sure you pack the moss tightly around your plants to help secure them in place.

Care and Maintenance: Water where it hangs by soaking with a hose every 10 to 14 days in the warm months and monthly during the winter. Water across the top of the wheel so that the water soaks the entire mossy area. Trim dead flowers and leaves. Fertilize twice a month during the summer with a liquid fertilizer. Add more succulents to your planting if any don't survive.

GLOSSARY

Caudiciform: A type of succulent plant that stores water in a fat, rooty stem protruding from the soil in a lump called a caudex.

Clumping: Forming a batch of the same plant from offsets.

Cresting: A succulent stem mutation that grows flat and wide and sends out unusual patterns of tightly packed rosettes along its misshapen trunk.

Dormant: A state of nongrowth when a plant reserves its energy during harsh weather.

Epiphyte: A plant that lives on other plants without feeding off them.

Hens and chicks: A type of succulent that has a central mother plant that grows many baby plants. The chicks are also known as offsets.

Horticultural charcoal: A grade of charcoal used for water management and drainage control in succulent container gardens and especially important for terrariums.

Leggy, legginess: Describes a plant that has an overly long stem, usually from growing toward faraway light, and results in raising its rosette up off the surface of the plant in a somewhat unattractive way.

Monocarpic: Describes a plant that flowers once and then dies.

Propagation: The process of growing new plants from an existing plant.

Pumice: A volcanic rock that serves as a supplement in succulent soil mixes to improve water drainage.

Specimen plant: The central focus plant of a design or landscape.

Stressed: A state of being that can occur when succulents are given less water, more sun or heat, or even more cold than they normally like, and which brings out pink, red, and purple colors in the plants' flesh.

Succulent: A plant that retains water in its leaves, stems, or roots.

Terrarium: An ecosystem enclosed in glass.

Variegated: A pattern of plant leaf color consisting of whites, creams, and yellows instead of the usual green.

Vertical garden: A type of garden created to be hung and grown on a fence or wall.

Xeriscape: A garden that grows and thrives with little or no irrigation.

INDEX

PHOTO INDEX

Houseleek 71
AKA HENS AND CHICKS
Sempervivum tectorum

Cobweb Sempervivum 72
AKA HENS AND CHICKS
Sempervivum arachnoideum

Queen of the Night 75
AKA DUTCHMAN'S PIPE CACTUS, NIGHT-BLOOMING CEREUS
Epiphyllum oxypetalum

Zebra Plant 76
Haworthia fasciata or *Haworthiopsis fasciata*

Cooper's Haworthia 79
AKA PUSSY FOOT, WINDOW HAWORTHIA
Haworthia cooperi var. *obtusa*

Horse's Teeth 80
Haworthia truncata

Little Warty 83
AKA COW TONGUE
Gasteria batesiana x *Gasteria "Old Man Silver"*

Ox Tongue 84
AKA DWARF TONGUE
Gasteria bicolor var. *Liliputana*

Aloe Vera 87
Aloe barbadensis

ACKNOWLEDGMENTS

Thanks to Rob, Dan, Seth, Harrison, Marie-Claire, Huck, Stephanie, Mariah, and Ai, the crew of Succulence, for outstanding support on every level.

Thanks to Flora Grubb for creating the first "lovely" nursery I fell for, to Debra Lee Baldwin for helping to ignite my passion for succulents, and to Salvador Mendoza, who grows amazing plants at Baja Cactus and Succulents.

Thanks to Allison Serrell for bringing me into this project, Rachel Weill for taking amazing photographs, Linda Lamb Peters for every level of photography support, and Elizabeth Castoria, Katie Moore, and everyone at Callisto Media.

Thanks to Denise and Anne for being the best sisters a middle brother could hope for.

Thanks to John Lucas for the mother ship connection and endless cheerleading, and Michael Stephens for being the plant wizard and introducing me to epiphyllum decades ago.

Thanks to Niffer Desmond, who gave me that first haworthia, and Darcy Lee for an amazing idea.

Thank you to Trudy for keeping me in stitches, Huckleberry for fundamental literary support, and Amy for the usual super everything she provides.

ABOUT THE AUTHOR

Ken Shelf is the owner of Succulence, a garden and lifestyle store in San
Francisco's Bernal Heights neighborhood.
Ken's love for succulents began with a
Haworthia fasciata he received as a gift
in 1994, and that he still has. Since then,
Ken has been exploring the mighty power
of succulents, their breathtaking beauty,
and their incredible will to live. Over the
past decade, he has taught numerous
classes and workshops on succulents and
vertical gardening. In addition, Ken creates masterful succulent centerpieces and
arrangements for special occasions and
provides custom landscaping and design
work throughout the Bay Area. Ken and
his wife, Amy, live in San Francisco with
their two teenagers. Ken has also written
a dozen plays, countless poems and song
lyrics, and a feature-length screenplay
that he directed and produced.